PRAISE FOR *THRIVE*

MW00412179

Powerful, generous, and person.... ....~ ~...~~~~~ guide and a workbook that will light the path for anyone who cares enough to make a difference.

—Seth Godin, *New York Times* best-selling
author of *Linchpin* and *The Purple Cow*

Thrive through the Five transforms challenges into positive opportunities and achievement. It's a must-read for school leaders.

—Jon Gordon, *New York Times* best-selling author of
The Energy Bus and *The Power of Positive Leadership*

One word: inspiring! What an audaciously and purposely written book. Anyone hoping to be challenged, to have their thinking pushed, and to be reminded of who they are and can be should read this book. Dr. Siler shares keys to successfully having goals and making them a reality while taking care of yourself and the people around you. No matter your profession or goals, *Thrive through the Five* helps you understand deeply who you are and who you can be during the hard moments. Simply amazing.

—LaDonna Monson Gulley, PhD, principal, Mesquite ISD,
and Raise Your Hand Texas alumna of Harvard
University's Art of Leadership Institute

A leader's leader, Dr. Jill Siler pours herself into this beautifully crafted book that encourages all of us to remember that the twelve most important inches of leadership are indeed those between the head and the heart. She pours herself into those she serves and uses her own powerful story to illustrate that who we are comes before what we do. Jill helps us find the courage and the competence to brave, grow, and thrive through the 5 percent of the job that challenges us. With practical truths, she invites us to move theory to practice and reminds us that leadership, at its best, is a calling.

—Ervin Knezek, EdD, founder, innovator, and
teacher, lead4ward, and author of *Be Bold*

Thrive through the Five is a revealing and powerful book that comes just as I am experiencing the biggest pandemic of my educational leadership career—COVID-19. We know leadership matters, and it definitely matters during a crisis. Jill's words are inspirational and instill hope and confidence to approach each issue, crisis, or even pandemic with the same fervor and strength. Every leader and aspiring leader should read this book.

—LaTonya Goffney, EdD, superintendent, Aldine ISD,
and 2017 Texas Superintendent of the Year

Thrive through the Five is a great story of one leader's journey to find a way through the parts of our jobs that don't always bring us the most joy, but often take up the most time. The quotes will inspire and the process will clearly help you navigate the 5 percent that has such an impact on our world both emotionally and physically as leaders.

—Joe Sanfelippo, PhD, superintendent, Fall Creek
School District, and author of *Hacking Leadership*

In *Thrive through the Five*, Jill Siler asks an inspiring question: "Can you imagine what joy our world would hold if every person loved what they did and was living to their fullest potential?" Throughout the book, with wisdom, practical advice, and vivid examples, Jill makes it possible for the reader to see that possibility for themselves. In her unique approach to addressing the specific 5 percent of one's job that is the most difficult, she masterfully provides hope in the hardest of places—light in the darkest corners—and ideas for how to overcome the challenges that stand in the way of success. Her book is sure to make a big impact on the readers who follow her lead.

—Joelle Jay, PhD, director, Leadership Research
Institute, and author of *The Inner Edge*

The collective leadership responsibilities of the public school superintendent are complex and thus not easily comprehended by all school district stakeholders. Dr. Siler's reflections on her

by superintendents and school boards, principals
ls, and the teachers who lead their grade levels,
and in their classrooms. *Thrive through the Five* is a
r educational leaders at all levels!

—**Miriam Ezzani, EdD**, assistant professor, educational
leadership, Texas Christian University

ever before, school and district leaders find themselves
unprecedented times. Although challenging, these
of uncertainty create opportunities for your leadership
Thrive through the Five, Siler provides a leadership
rk, complete with tangible strategies and action steps,
lead through, in, and back out of those moments that
ge us to our core.

—**Thomas C. Murray**, director of innovation, Future Ready
Schools, and author of *Personal & Authentic*

I first discovered the blog maintained by Jill Siler in her role as
erintendent, I realized I had encountered someone who truly
es the chance to change young lives in her community—even
n the obstacles might be severe and off-putting at times. That
g is required monthly reading for me, and now many others
benefit from the affirmation and expressions of hope and joy
e carries forward in her first book, *Thrive through the Five*.

—**Jay P. Goldman**, editor, *School Administrator* magazine,
published by AASA, the School Superintendents Association

Dr. Siler has written an engaging, informative book with advice
and suggestions on how to thrive, not just survive, the 5 percent
of challenging times that make leadership so difficult. However,
after reading her book, I believe it is as much about powerful living
as it is about powerful leading. Yes, this book will enhance your
leadership skills, but even more importantly, it will enrich your life
as you navigate the challenging times of today.

—**Sandra Harris, PhD**, professor emerita (ret.), educational
leadership, Lamar University, and author of *Learning from the Best*

leadership journey a
challenges of this ho
messages are enjoya
especially inspirational
leaders. This book is a m

—Rubén Olivárez,

More than
navigating
moments
legacy.
framewo
for us t
challen

Jill Siler not only shares her
strategies to lead through sea
ever, *Thrive through the Five* is a
want to rise up and learn to nav
create new and better opportuniti

—Katie Martin, PhD, vice pres
Altitude Learning, and author o

"Heavy is the head that wears the crow
quoted to me during a crisis when I was
Little did I know when I entered that role
school district could be so high in one mom
be so agonizing in the next. Leaders are n
times but by the challenges they help their co
In *Thrive through the Five*, Dr. Siler uses her o
expertise to provide practical, relevant insights
leaders can thrive in those difficult times. This s
reading for anyone who dares to be a great lead

—Kevin Brown, EdD, executive
Association of School

Dr. Jill Siler, a current superintendent, shares her pow
on leadership! She tells her personal and professi
with grace and wisdom and weaves in solutions for
problems of practice that are too often encountered in
Each chapter ends with effective tips and an opportu
reflection. These lessons are applicable to leadership pr

encountered
leading scho
departments
must-read fo

Wher
a su
relis
whe
blo
wil
sh

This book reads as though you are sitting across the table at a coffee shop, gaining wisdom from an incredible leader and mentor. In *Thrive through the Five*, Jill does a masterful job of using stories to share practical steps and tools to maneuver through the difficult aspects of the leadership journey. Often, authors only use stories of success to deliver valuable lessons. In this leadership manifesto, Jill's transparency guides through failure, fear, stress, and high-pressure situations to inspire, empower, and enhance your leadership capacity. This is a brilliant book for any leader, regardless of your experience, and it will have a profound impact on how you thrive in your school, district, and community!

—**Joshua Stamper**, assistant principal, speaker, and host of *Aspire: The Leadership Development Podcast*

THRIVE THROUGH THE FIVE

DR. JILL M. SILER

THRIVE THROUGH THE FIVE

PRACTICAL TRUTHS TO POWERFULLY LEAD THROUGH CHALLENGING TIMES

Thrive through the Five: Practical Truths to Powerfully Lead through Challenging Times
© 2020 Jill M. Siler

This book is available at special discounts when purchased in quantity for educational purposes or as premiums, promotions, or fundraisers. For inquiries and details, contact the publisher at books@daveburgessconsulting.com.

Published by Dave Burgess Consulting, Inc.
San Diego, CA
DaveBurgessConsulting.com

Library of Congress Control Number: 2020941073
Paperback ISBN: 978-1-951600-38-9
Ebook ISBN: 978-1-951600-39-6

Image of gazelle © Tawatchai Khid-arn, Dreamstime.com, ID 70327482
Image of iceberg © MethMehr, Dreamstime.com, ID 140063532
Photograph of Fort Pitt Tunnel by Bruce Cridlebaugh (pghbridges.com). Used with permission.
Photograph of skyline of downtown Pittsburgh at twilight, istockphoto.com; F11, 589133716. Used with permission.
#ArmMeWithBooks image via Lindsey Paull, Instagram: @missjohnstonsjourney. Used with permission.

Cover image by Laci Bracewell
Interior design by Liz Schreiter
Sketchnote designs by Amelia Buchanan
Editing and production by Reading List Editorial: readinglisteditorial.com

This book is dedicated to the people who first taught me how to thrive in any situation—my mom and dad. The love and support you have shown, coupled with the life lessons you have taught me, have made me who I am today. And to the people who love me through every mountaintop and valley I traverse: my incredible husband, William, and our amazing kids, Caitlyn and Caleb—you all make every moment of life worth living for!

CONTENTS

INTRODUCTION:
I *L-O-V-E* LOVE MY JOB

*If you do what you love, you'll never
work a day in your life.*

—MARC ANTHONY

*I absolutely love what I do, and it is
the hardest work I've ever done.*

—JILL M. SILER

love my job, like, *L-O-V-E* love my job as a school superintendent! I
recently visited a precious friend who is a missionary overseas. As
we were catching up on all aspects of life, she asked me this very question: "What do you love about your job?"

So. Many. Things.

I love that there is purpose inherently in what I do. I don't have
to make connections—it is visible each and every day as I see young
people (and not so young people) learning, growing, and becoming
better versions of themselves. I love that I get to set the tone and
foster a positive culture within our school community. I love that I get
to work with incredible campus leaders and up-and-coming leaders.
I love that I get to partner with superintendents across the state to

do better and be better for kids. I love that I have seven of the most committed, kid-focused board members who are all working toward our shared vision. I love being a small part of making school *great* for kids. I. Love. My. Job.

I often share with people, though, that while I love my job 95 percent of the time—there is this other 5 percent. The 5 percent no one likes to talk about, but which is ever present in the work we do as school leaders (probably in the work that everyone does). The 95 percent of what I do is *so* great, but that 5 percent can be absolutely horrible. The 5 percent is:

- the tragedy that impacts the school community;
- the aftermath when any human in the building (young or not as young) makes a poor choice;
- the aftermath when *we* as leaders make a poor choice, handle a situation ineffectively, or let someone down with our words and actions;
- the negative viral social media post about something that happened at school (that may or may not be factual);
- the unavailability of funds to provide everything our awesome staff deserves;
- the inability to defend ourselves in situations because we are unable (and it would be inappropriate) to share confidential information;
- the pressure we face when we have to go on camera or on stage;
- the weight (let me just pause there for a moment . . . the *weight*) of hundreds of people's livelihoods resting on our decision-making and leadership.

OK, can I change my 95-to-5 ratio? you might be thinking. To be perfectly honest, I've had seasons where it has been a solid 95 to 5 and seasons where the ratio was very different.

And I don't think leaders are the only ones who face this. As I remember my years in the classroom, I absolutely *loved* my job then, too. I loved being able to make a tangible difference in the lives of kids each and every day. I loved that my room was my sanctuary—it was a safe place for kids to learn, grow, take risks, and have fun. And I loved that it was also MY place to learn, grow, take risks, and have fun, too! I loved that my students needed to master curriculum standards, yet I had so much autonomy to design learning experiences for them. I loved teaching a subject that allowed for daily connections to real life (ninth-grade world geography). I loved the age group I taught—mature enough for life-changing conversations about the world, but young enough to still be silly and innocent. I loved connecting with them through the sport I coached and the clubs I sponsored. I loved pep rallies on Fridays and Homecomings in the fall and graduations in the spring. I loved seeing my students flourish after graduation and treasured their visits when they came back to see me. I. Loved. My. Job.

But there is a 5 percent in this work, too. The 5 percent is:

- the tragedy that impacts one of our students or their families;
- the aftermath when one of our students makes a poor choice;
- the aftermath when *we* make a poor choice, handle a situation ineffectively, or let a student down with our words and actions;
- the negative viral social media posts about us, our assignments, or grades;
- the unavailability of funds to do everything our awesome students deserve;
- the challenging parent who makes us question why we do what we do;
- all of the "stuff" that is above and beyond the hours we spend teaching (attendance, grading, parent communication, preparing for student/parent conferences, professional development, remediation with students, etc.);
- the pressure we face, and we know our students are feeling, when it comes time for standardized tests;

- the loss of autonomy in the classroom when the pendulum swings to scripted lessons and assessments;
- the weight (let me just pause there for a moment . . . the *weight*) of students' well-being resting on our decision-making and classroom leadership.

We all have to deal with that small percentage of our work (and life) when things are really, really hard. So how do we do that? The goal of this book is to help us not just survive those moments, days, and seasons, but to THRIVE! This work is to help us lead through the really difficult times in a way where the 5 percent doesn't overshadow the 95 percent of what we really love.

- Part I (Chapters 1–3) tackles some of the underlying or contributing factors in our 5 percent. Sometimes the difficult moments in our work and lives are due to specific events or crises, but sometimes the 5 percent is happening because of our own struggles with issues like failure, fear, or increasing expectations and pressure. Part I talks about **Leading Through**, how we lead through some of the difficult personal matters that plague each of us in our work and in our lives.
- Part II (Chapters 4–7) moves inward and speaks to strategies that help us be our best through the 5 percent *and* the 95 percent. This includes ensuring that not only are we leading and developing others but also that we ourselves are being led and taking care of ourselves. We will talk about how to deal with feelings of being overwhelmed or even inadequate that naturally come as we push ourselves into new levels of responsibility and leadership and how and when to make a change in our work or lives. Part II talks about **Leading In**, the internal strategies to leadership and life that help us be at 100 percent so that we can most effectively lead through the 5 percent and the 95 percent.
- Part III (Chapters 8–14) touches on external strategies for thriving through the 5 percent. These are the specific and tangible

strategies we can employ when facing a challenging issue or season. We will tackle how to ground our perspective when things get tough as well as how to work through messy situations and decisions. We will talk about how to inspire hope in the darkest moments, how to engage with others around contentious issues, and how to lead from a place of vision in moments when we ourselves might be floundering. Part III discusses **Leading Out**, how we outwardly lead through difficult times.

Each chapter begins with a quote that addresses the theme of the chapter and some words around personal struggles and learning in that area. We then transition to tangible strategies in a **Practical Truths to Powerfully Lead** section. While I hope that the stories and experiences shared will connect and resonate, these condensed practical truths are designed to give us new perspective on the challenging parts of what we do. Next, there are **5 Tips to Thrive** outlining strategies we can implement immediately to help us truly thrive through the 5 percent moments.

Each chapter then closes with a **Framework to Thrive**, which are action steps leading us through purposeful questions and discovery around our own journeys. I would encourage all of us to take time to reflect on our own stories and experiences around each theme and then share our thoughts and learning with someone else. There is power in reflecting on and sharing the growth we've made in each of our journeys. So, let's be brave, unleash our biggest dreams, and get ready to embrace our new bold selves!

Can you imagine what joy our world would hold if every person loved what they did and was living to their fullest potential? My hope is that this book helps each of us realize that no matter what we do, everyone has a portion of their work and life that is really difficult. But the better we can be at leading through the 5 percent that we may dread at times, the more we'll delight in the 95 percent we love!

FRAMEWORK TO THRIVE: I LOVE MY JOB

What do you LOVE about your job? (your 95 percent)

What are the challenging parts about what you do? (your 5 percent)

What are some strategies that help you get through the really difficult parts of your work and life?

We all have parts of our work and lives that we LOVE and parts that are really challenging. How does this understanding help you think about thriving in the 5 percent?

PART I
LEADING THROUGH . . .

- How can we lead through difficult and messy things like failure, fear, and heightened expectations?

- What are the underlying factors that contribute to the 5 percent of our work and life that is really difficult?

- How do we lead through these underlying factors in order to thrive through the most difficult 5 percent of what we do?

Sometimes places like failure, fear, and faith are the very places from which greatness, hope, and success are born.

ONE

FAILURE IS PART OF IT

Far better is it to dare mighty things, to win glorious triumphs, even though checkered by failure . . . than to rank with those poor spirits who neither enjoy nor suffer much, because they live in a gray twilight that knows not victory nor defeat.

—THEODORE ROOSEVELT

I remember my very first keynote as an up-and-coming leader. I had given presentations and led sessions at various conferences, but this was the first time I addressed the whole audience, and I remember apologizing as I began my speech because I was going to start by discussing failure. Fast-forward fifteen years later, and I had my first TED Talk–like event. Again, I started with failure. And now, given this incredible opportunity to write my first book . . . I'm starting with failure.

Why would I do that? Because too often we think of success as a destination—the place toward which we strive. But really, success is found in the journey. And that journey doesn't actually look like some pristine FastPass to greatness, but rather a rugged trek through hard places, places like failure and fear and disappointment and struggle. If we're going to thrive through the 5 percent, we have to learn how to work through fear and how to accept failure as a part of our learning journey and a tool to prime and prepare us for success.

I think we struggle with this notion because society presents a different truth. As we scroll through social media, we are bombarded with the best thirty seconds of everyone's lives—whether personally or professionally. And when *our* lives don't measure up with the false impression given from the accumulation of these networks, we begin to doubt. And I don't think I'm alone. I don't think I'm the only one who plays it safe, who doubts their abilities and battles with fear, who's afraid to fail, and who is convinced that everyone else is better than, smarter than, more accomplished than they are. Even as I started putting together these thoughts around thriving in the 5 percent, first as a blog in 2019 and now as a book in 2020, I worried about giving a false impression in this work. Because the reality is that sometimes it is not a 95-to-5 split. Honestly, I've had years where if I got to 75-to-25, I'd call it a win.

But failure is a real part of struggling in the 5 percent. I don't know anyone who has made perfect decisions every day, who never made a mistake, who bypassed seasons of growth because they were naturally equipped for every job they took. The bottom line about leadership is that you don't know what you don't know. So, there will be mistakes and there will be failures. To be the best version of ourselves and truly enjoy all of what we do, we need to know how to lead through failure.

I learned about failure at an early age. If there is one defining physical characteristic about my female self, it is the fact that I am tall—and grew up tall. Any women readers who are, say, five ten and taller will be able to relate to the very real challenges of being tall: finding clothes, buying shoes, and (let's just put it out there!) finding a husband.

Another thing that came with the territory of being tall was the presumption that height equated to athletic giftedness. Not only did I play sports, but surely I must play them well. Of course, the first sport my parents and coaches thought I would be good at was basketball. So, I tried playing basketball in elementary school. I tried in middle school. I tried in high school. Don't get me wrong—I totally *tried*! But, in a word, I was *horrible*. Not just bad, not mediocre—horrible.

Years later, when my mom and I were reflecting on my basketball days and realizing now how tall I was then, I thought for sure I had missed my calling. Maybe if I had just given it a few more years or had a different coach or team, I could have been great. I shared that with my mom, and she chuckled and said that the only word she could think of in describing me on a basketball court was *gazelle*. All legs and hopping all over the place with no rhyme or reason. I wasn't sure what a gazelle looked like, so I recently googled it, and, well . . .

But as a kid I learned quickly. "If at first you don't succeed, try and try again," the old adage goes. And so I did. If I was not good on the basketball court, then my height must be an asset somewhere else. So on to volleyball I went. Clearly tall people are needed for that! If nothing else, I should be able to stand in front, put my arms up, and block the ball.

Playing volleyball in the eighties was totally different than today. Our athletes today play on these custom-made courts with fancy nets that are literally drilled into the ground. Back when I played, we also had nets, but they were connected to poles soldered to massive round bases that you literally rolled onto the court and set into place.

So here I am playing volleyball (in the front of course, because I'm tall) and the ball comes my way. I go up for the hit, and my hand makes contact with the ball (which, let's be clear, is an anomaly). I was so determined to get the ball to the ground that I put tremendous follow-through into it . . . So much follow-through that I fell into the net and took it to the floor along with those thousand-pound bases. I literally could have killed someone in that moment! But I continued to learn important lessons, like this one from Confucius: "Our greatest glory is not in never falling, but in rising every time we fall." I'm sure the great philosopher didn't mean this in the literal sense in which I am interpreting it, but this truth holds here, too!

I won't bore you with my entire middle school athletic career, but I will share some highlights. I ran track in middle school—a hurdler, as I was supposed to be good at that with my long legs. In my first race, my foot caught the top of the hurdle and down I went, pulling it on top of me. I played softball and was cut from the sixth-grade team. (Is it even legal to have cuts to a sixth-grade team?) My soccer career involved a lot of bench-sitting, which isn't exactly notable. And I hate to admit it, but this awkward, clumsy, six-foot-plus preteen even tried cheerleading. I am certain that there are some lovely six-foot cheerleaders who are both graceful and cute. I was not one of them.

Let's get real and talk about failure for a moment. Thomas Edison once said, "Many of life's failures are people who did not realize how close they were to success when they gave up." This was so true of me. Had I let the athletic failures of my childhood dictate the athletic future of my high school and college years, I would have missed out on one of the greatest blessings in my life—swimming.

I did not begin swimming until my sophomore year of high school. I won't say that my talent for swimming was instantaneous or that this new sport was easy, but I fell in love with the water and found I had the passion and potential to be successful. I followed this dream and was able to swim at the Division I level at the University of Pittsburgh.

I placed in the top three at the Big East Championships year after year and was an Academic All-American. My senior year my name was engraved in the Varsity Walk of Fame, alongside names like Mike Ditka, Tony Dorsett, and Dan Marino, as one of the Senior Athletes of the Year. Failure prepares us for success!

I will admit that it is easy to laugh at silly athletic failures from childhood. It is altogether different to talk about adult failures in our professional work.

I remember my very first superintendent interview. I was blown away even to get the call. The district was *way* out of my league—large, high performing, and located in a beautiful area of our state. Any sitting superintendent in the state could and should have been asked to interview for that district, yet they called me, an executive director in a successful, growing district, as one of six to come in for an interview.

I put everything I had into it. I knew that district backward and forward—every challenge they were facing and every accomplishment they had achieved. I knew every board member by name and occupation. In a word, I was prepared. The interview started, and the board members began to ask questions—one by one around the table. And I answered. Question. Answer. Question. Answer. Question. Answer. They asked their final question. There had been twenty-one in total. I glanced at the clock and saw that only twenty-one minutes had passed. Just so we're all on the same page—in the interviewing world, that is *not* a good sign.

I walked out of that interview not knowing whether to laugh or cry. When the search firm's representative called a few days later, I immediately began to apologize. I felt like I hadn't represented them well, kind of "embarrassed the family," if you will. He quickly responded: "No, Jill—they really liked you! In fact, they said you had 'great energy.'"

I had to chuckle to myself. Of *course* they thought I had great energy—who answers twenty-one questions in twenty-one minutes?!?

The world would look at that interview as a failure. I'll be honest: I looked at that interview initially as a failure. I clearly did not get the job. But this, too, was a success. It was an opportunity for me to learn, to practice, to grow, to reflect, and to *be better*.

WE ARE DEFINED BY OUR FAILURES ONLY IF WE LET OURSELVES BE. FAIL. LEARN FROM IT. BE BETTER.

Six months later, I had another opportunity to interview for a superintendent position, this time for Gunter ISD, a small district about an hour north of Dallas, Texas.

So much had changed in those six months. I shifted from a place of being *prepared* to being *ready*. I shifted from a place of understanding that my job was not just to answer the *what*, or the "head" part of their questions, but to speak to the *why* and the *how*, the "heart" part of their questions. I needed to dive deep below the surface and answer their questions from a place of values and beliefs, from a place of purpose.

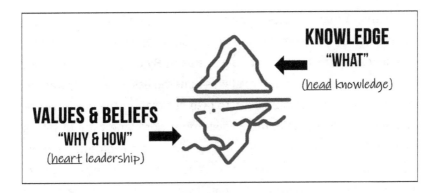

I studied and prepared the same way I did in my first interview, but I also began to look at questions more closely, to find the greater meaning of what they were asking. If they were asking how I evaluated staff, no longer did I talk about the "tool" (in our state, PDAS or T-TESS). I focused on how I helped people recognize where they were in the context of where they wanted to be (or where we needed them to be), and how I helped support them toward improvement. In response to every single question, I shared stories illustrating *what* I had been doing, *how* I had been doing it, and *why* I was doing it in the first place. I connected *my* passion and skills with *their* goals and needs.

After two interviews spanning three and a half hours, I was named lone finalist for Gunter ISD. I wasn't named lone finalist at Gunter ISD because I simply had "a good day" or "a good interview." I got the job because I had an opportunity to learn and fail previously in the interview process. It was that initial failure that prepared me for eventual success.

Part of leading through really difficult moments is finding a way to learn, grow, and lead through failure.

PRACTICAL TRUTHS TO POWERFULLY LEAD THROUGH FAILURE

Failure Is Part of It

There are so many stories I could tell. I've made mistakes as a classroom teacher, as a campus administrator, as a central office leader, and now as a superintendent—*big* mistakes. By the grace of God, not career-ending mistakes, but mistakes nonetheless. If we truly want to be the best version of ourselves, to take our craft to the next level, or to advance in leadership, that growth does not come without taking risks and facing failure along the way. We have to reframe how we look at failure and understand that it is not something we just endure, it is *the* thing that can make us great. If we want to love 95 percent of what we do, we have to, as former Green Beret Chris Dessi states, "get comfortable with being uncomfortable" and accept that failure is part of growing.[1]

The Line to Success Is Not Straight

I joked about the "if at first you don't succeed, try and try again" adage, but it is the truth. In the job leading up to my leap to the superintendency, it was adversity that prompted my jump. Even if we are not moving in the seamless, straight trajectory we had anticipated or hoped for, it doesn't mean that we are not ready and equipped to be successful in our next steps. The line to success is rarely straight, so if we are not feeling like we're poised for success, it may take a leap, but we can find the right job in the right place. The trajectory is ours to design and to walk. Don't be afraid to write your own script.

JUST BECAUSE YOU ARE NOT MOVING IN A SEAMLESS, STRAIGHT TRAJECTORY YOU HAD ANTICIPATED OR HOPED FOR, IT DOESN'T MEAN THAT YOU ARE NOT READY OR EQUIPPED TO BE SUCCESSFUL IN YOUR NEXT STEPS.

1   In "How to Get Comfortable with Being Uncomfortable," published on Inc. on November 15, 2016, Chris Dessi summarizes his conversation with a Green Beret, in which they discuss "embracing the suck" and other strategies. Check it out: https://www.inc.com/chris-dessi/how-to-get-comfortable-with-being-uncomfortable-according-to-a-green-beret.html.

Failure Is Where Learning and Growth Happen

When I was a first-year campus administrator, I took on the task of updating our employee handbook. I did what every good leader does: I reviewed exemplar handbooks from many other districts and used the best parts of each to inform ours. The finished product was fantastic! Or so I thought, until our first employee went on family medical leave and I realized I had inadvertently copied another district's leave policy without consulting our own. Our district honored the policy I had accidentally included and covered the financial loss, which was significant. I was fortunate to have a campus principal who cared about me as a leader, so he made sure I understood the magnitude of the mistake, then told me I was an incredible leader and not to make the same mistake again. I, in turn, accepted full responsibility, reviewed every other document I had revised that year, and triple-checked policy in the rest of that particular handbook.

Twenty years later, that one failure still informs my work. When we refuse to accept responsibility for our own failures, we lose the opportunity to grow and learn and become better. Best-selling leadership author Jon Gordon calls this the difference between "those who fail and those who fail forward."[2] Learning and growth happen in the midst of failure—but only if we let them.

LEARNING AND GROWTH HAPPEN IN THE MIDST OF FAILURE—BUT ONLY IF WE LET THEM.

---

2   Jon Gordon, "Failing Forward," April 2, 2018, http://www.jongordon.com/positivetip/failing-forward.html.

Resiliency research shows the same. Educational researchers John Fleming and Robert Ledogar noted that "further research has led to the concepts of resilient reintegration, whereby a confrontation with adversity can lead for some to a new level of growth, and, for some, to the notion that resilience is something innate that needs only to be properly awakened."[3] Coming face-to-face with adversity leads to a new level of growth, and even if we don't think we have the resiliency to withstand it, it is inherent in us. It just needs to be awakened.

Failure Is Only Part of the Story

Failure is temporary; it is rarely the end of the story. Best-selling author Brené Brown talks about failing brilliantly: "Failure is an imperfect word because, if you take the time and have the patience to learn from your failures, then they aren't failures any longer—they're lessons."[4] We are only defined by our failures if we let ourselves be. Fail, learn from it, and be better.

Conclusion

The question is not whether we will face failure: each of us will face adversity in our work and in our lives. We will all fail. The question is, how will we respond? Jon Gordon puts it best: "[Failure] gives you a test designed to measure your courage, perseverance, commitment and dedication. Are you a pretender who gives up after a little adversity or a contender who keeps getting up after getting knocked down?"[5] The next time you fail, take a second to grieve your ego. Take a few moments to determine what went wrong. And then get up and get out there and try again. Failure is an event, not a sentence.

---

3   John Fleming and Robert Ledogar, "Resilience, an Evolving Concept: A Review of Literature Relevant to Aboriginal Research," Summer 2008, https://www. ncbi.nlm.nih.gov/pmc/articles/PMC2956753.

4   Howard Tullman, "3 Tips From Brené Brown about Failing Brilliantly," Inc., September 8, 2015, https://www.inc.com/howard -tullman-3-tips-from-brene-brown-about-failing-brilliantly.html.

5   Jon Gordon, "The Gift of Failure," October 18, 2013, http://www.jongordon. com/positive-tip-gift-of-failure.html.

5 TIPS TO THRIVE

1 Identify the mistake and the moment you went wrong. Determine why the situation was a failure and what you can learn from it so it won't happen again.

2 Own it. I don't know that I can say it any more clearly. Accountability requires taking responsibility for one's actions, so own what is yours to own. And honestly, leadership is about taking responsibility for all actions—even when they're not your own.

3 Make amends. Two of the most powerful words we have in our vocabulary are *I'm sorry*. Avoid a vague "I'm sorry this situation happened" or "I'm sorry this outcome happened." Take ownership and apologize specifically for what happened.

4 Look to a quality leader for mentorship. The more open you are to feedback around your own performance, the faster you will hone your leadership skills.

5 Don't dwell. Perhaps this is much easier said than done, but there is a vast difference between owning a mistake versus dwelling on a failure. Address those who are concerned, do your best to make amends, ignore the haters, and move on.[6]

---

6 I have to give major props on this whole section to the brilliant Rebecca Egger. She is a former teacher and photographer with a million gifts who did some beta reading for me and shared that it would be helpful to give some tangible tips at the end of each chapter. She even started this specific list as an example, sharing her own takeaways from this chapter.

Far better it is to dare mighty things, to win glorious triumphs, even though checkered by failure... than to rank with those poor spirits who neither enjoy nor suffer much, because they live in a gray twilight that knows not victory nor defeat.
—Theodore Roosevelt

Failure Is Part of It

Thrive Through the Five by Jill M. Siler

Failure Is Part of It

Reframe how we look at failure.

The Line to Success Is Not Straight

Success

Failure Is Where Learning and Growth Happen

Failure — Failure — Failure

Failure Is only Part of the Story

Fail. Learn from it. Be Better.

we are only defined by our failures if we let ourselves be it

Learning and growth happen in the midst of failure – but only if we let them.

sketchnote by Amelia Buchanan
@edtech_amelia

FRAMEWORK TO THRIVE: FAILURE

What is one failure you've had or mistake you've made?	How did you learn from it personally?	How does it impact the way you lead today?
see attached doc		

Describe a juncture along your path where your line wasn't straight, but you still found success in the end.

How does the understanding that failure is part of learning and growing help you think about thriving in the 5 percent?

The 5% is

T W O

LEARNING TO DANCE WITH FEAR

I learned that courage was not the absence of fear, but the triumph over it. The brave man is not he who does not feel afraid, but he who conquers that fear.

—NELSON MANDELA

One of my greatest passions is working with up-and-coming leaders, and I've had the great privilege of presenting at the Aspiring Superintendent Academy at our state's educational leadership conference for the past several years. Each year I start with the same slide . . . a slide of confessions. If we're going to be honest, these were the thoughts that kept me awake at night as I contemplated a move into the superintendency.

- **I didn't feel like I was ready.** To put it more clearly, I didn't think I could do the job. This was not an inappropriate fear, mind you. I could count on one hand the number of board meetings I had sat through from start to finish. I knew a lot in the areas of curriculum, instruction and assessment, campus operations, and HR, but was woefully unprepared in areas like working with the board, school finance, transportation, and maintenance. The same could be said when I took my first campus leadership position—and my first teaching position, for that matter! Nothing prepares us for the job like actually taking the job. So, we are never going to feel totally ready for something new.

- **I didn't want to move away from "home."** We had lived in the same community for sixteen years and didn't want to leave our friends, family, and church home. My kids were already in school and were happy, plus we loved the area where we lived. I was anxious about uprooting my whole family for a job I wasn't entirely certain I could do (or would even like), and I worried whether our family could be happy anywhere else.

- **I worried about whether I would like the job.** I knew enough to know that the work was hard. But I also knew enough to know that the work could be ugly. This is where my story of the 95 to 5 began: I tell people that I love my job 95 percent of the time. That sounds (and is!) great, but what people don't know is how bad the 5 percent can be. I was deeply worried that the 5 percent would overshadow the 95 percent.

- **I worried that I couldn't balance being a mom and a superintendent.** My kids were three and seven when I became a superintendent. My toddler son literally ran laps around the venue at our welcome reception. I worried about disappointing my children and family, disappointing my district, or—worse—disappointing everyone. I had many great role models who were superintendents, but none that looked like me, a young mom with young kids. And that made me question whether I *could* or *should* even be doing this work.

All of those thoughts were **fear**.

I have been thinking deeply about failure and fear this past year, and there are many differences between them. But the most significant difference is this:

- Failure is hard, but it happens. It literally happens. And then it is over. And yes, you may face consequences. But you learn, you grow, you reflect, and you become better. It is an event. It might be a private event or it might be a public event, but it is an event and therefore finite in nature.

Fear, though . . .

- Fear can be constant. It is that ever-present "what if." What if I don't meet expectations? What if I am not successful? What if the worst possible outcome comes to fruition?

Fear can be debilitating. It can be crippling. And it can paralyze us in our work. I was taking notes in church one Sunday morning, and the message was about how when we really commit to moving forward, there will often be attempts to derail us. Our pastor made a point of saying, "Our mission sometimes walks us through the 'valley of the shadow of doubt.'" Did you catch that? I chuckled when I did. He didn't misspeak; I miswrote. It is the "valley of the shadow of death," not doubt, yet *doubt* is what I heard. But what happens so often is that fear leads to doubt, and doubt leads to inaction, and inaction leads to death.

We doubt and don't act, and we doubt and don't act, and we doubt and don't act—until our greatest hopes and dreams might as well be dead. This is fear, and we cannot let it take hold in our lives. The line from that great psalmist is "Even though I walk through the valley of the shadow of death, I will fear no evil, for You are with me."[1] Doubt is born from fear and can lead to the death of some wonderful experiences and events in our lives.

Fear is something I have struggled with not only recently; it is a battle I have fought for years—decades, in fact. I yearn to not struggle with fear and have read books and articles and listened to speakers about this very topic. I even resorted to Google: *How to get rid of fear?* I discovered a blog post by the writer and entrepreneur Seth Godin— and it was actually titled, "How Do I Get Rid of the Fear?" I clicked with anticipation, knowing that I was finally going to find my answer. Here was his response:

---

1 Psalm 23

Alas, this is the wrong question.

The only way to get rid of the fear is to stop doing things that might not work, to stop putting yourself out there, to stop doing work that matters.

FEAR LEADS TO DOUBT, AND DOUBT LEADS TO INACTION, AND INACTION LEADS TO DEATH. WE DOUBT AND DON'T ACT UNTIL OUR GREATEST HOPES AND DREAMS MIGHT AS WELL BE DEAD. **THIS IS FEAR, AND WE CANNOT LET IT TAKE HOLD IN OUR LIVES.**

Let me just pause here. Is *any* part of that OK with any of you? That you would stop doing things that might not work—in other words, never take a risk again? That you would stop putting yourself out there—to never really go for anything or stand for anything? That you'd stop doing work that matters? Absolutely not! And Seth would agree. He goes on to say:

> No, the right question is, "How do I dance with the fear?"
> Fear is not the enemy. Paralysis is the enemy.[2]

You might be reading this thinking, *This is the most depressing book ever! Where are we going with this?* Where we're going is this: If there is one quote I could recite over and over again, it would be Bruce Lee's statement that "courage isn't the absence of fear. It is the ability to act in the presence of fear."

---

2   Seth Godin, "How Do I Get Rid of the Fear?" April 20, 2014, https://seths. blog/2014/04/how-do-i-get-rid-of-the-fear/.

When I'm in a place of fear, the questions I ask revolve around this one: Am I being called?

- Am I being called to move through this situation?
- Am I being called to act in this situation?
- Am I being called to lead through this situation?

And if the answer is yes, then I act. Even in the midst of fear. The goal isn't to eradicate fear. The goal is to lead through it anyway.

THE GOAL ISN'T TO ERADICATE FEAR. THE GOAL IS TO LEAD THROUGH IT ANYWAY.

Even now, in my eighth year as a superintendent, I still battle fear. I battle worries that I'm not doing enough for my district, for my family, for myself, for (*fill in the blank*). I struggle with fear and anxiety around public speaking—which, by the way, is kind of what I do for a living. And to be really honest, the same fears I battled eight years ago when contemplating the next steps in my professional journey, I battle now as I contemplate what's to come in my professional career. I have so many thoughts about what I want to do and how I want to be, but sometimes I can become paralyzed by fear.

So many things in my 5 percent, and maybe yours, too, come down to fear. The upcoming contentious meeting with an employee or parent; the worry of a tragedy happening that, regardless the level of preparation, you're not prepared for; facing the next unfamiliar situation where you'll question which decisions are right and best for kids—the list goes on. When we're able to act and lead in the midst of the fear, our 5 percent becomes more bearable.

PRACTICAL TRUTHS TO POWERFULLY LEAD THROUGH FEAR

Everyone Has Fear. Acknowledge It.

One thing I've learned as I've shared my fears with aspiring leaders is that everyone thinks they're the only one with doubts and fears. You are not alone. The more I have been open about it, the more empowered my colleagues have become to talk about and face their own fears. Fear is not some man-made figment of our imagination. If you've ever walked on stage, into a contentious meeting, or into an interview for a job you really wanted, you know the very real physical response that fear brings. So, acknowledge it. Brené Brown talks about leaning into your fears instead of backing away. Referring to her critics, she shared, "Expect that they'll be there, in the front row seats" and then do what you do anyway.[3] Fear is a natural human reaction to any action outside of our comfort zone. Expect it, acknowledge it, and lead through it.

THE MORE WE TALK ABOUT OUR FEAR WITH ONE ANOTHER, THE MORE EMPOWERED WE BECOME. EVERYONE HAS FEAR. EXPECT IT, ACKNOWLEDGE IT, AND LEAD THROUGH IT.

---

3   Aimee Groth, "How a TED Speaker Learned to Ignore Her Critics," Business Insider, March 27, 2013, https://www.businessinsider.com/brene-brown-how -to-deal-with-fear-2013-5.

Decide How Much Weight to Give It

As we were getting ready to roll out our new school year last fall, I found myself with a heavy heart over something school related. I confided with a colleague about my worries, and she shared the most profound statement back to me: "Jill, you get to decide how much weight you give this." There are issues in life where we don't get to decide (matters of life and death, a tragedy that impacts the school, etc.), but for much of the 5 percent, we really do get to decide how much weight to give things. Understand the issue, dig deep into the details, then step back and look at the big picture—understand where it falls in the overall context of life, and adjust the weight you give it accordingly.

UNDERSTAND WHERE THE ISSUE FALLS IN THE OVERALL CONTEXT OF LIFE. THEN ADJUST THE WEIGHT YOU GIVE IT ACCORDINGLY.

Just Begin

The easiest way for fear to paralyze us is through inaction. When we focus on the expanse between where we are and where we want to be, we can freeze up. Dale Carnegie noted that "inaction breeds doubt and fear. Action breeds confidence and courage. If you want to conquer fear, do not sit home and think about it. Go out and get busy."[4]

---

4   Dale Carnegie was an American author and lecturer who authored several books including *How to Win Friends and Influence People* (1936). This is a quote that has been attributed to him.

Don't worry about achieving the end goal. Focus on the next best step that will advance you toward that end.

I struggle with this a lot. I think I should be able to move from where I am to where I want to be in one fell swoop. But really, what I need to do is simply take the next best step. If you have a desire in your heart to write a book, the first step isn't to start your manuscript. Instead, how about meeting with someone who's actually written a book and having a conversation about how they did it and what they learned along the way? Or start sharing thoughts on your subject in a blog or a series of articles. Or (you've probably picked up that I am preaching to myself at this point) how about we just shift our activity on Twitter from consuming to producing? How about we just start with 280 characters? I got past the paralysis that comes from thinking solely about the end goal, the *there's no way I could do that* thought, through small beginning steps.

I had the chance this past year to visit my former hometown's church. Before I moved, I was part of the group that helped bring in our new pastor. I enjoyed seeing how God was at work in my church family before I left, and now eight years later. The pastor had no idea I would be there that morning, yet he must have known, because his message seemed specifically designed for Jill Siler. Have you ever had a message just grab you by your soul? So many ideas, hopes, and dreams that had been hiding in my deepest thoughts were given permission to come out. My mind was spinning.

After the message, I told the pastor how good it was to see him. And I shared that I couldn't *ever* come to hear him again. He laughed. I told him I was serious. The last time I was under his teaching, I ended up moving to the other side of the state and taking this crazy awesome job as a superintendent. And now, after another message from him, I'd unearthed all of these crazy awesome thoughts about what was to come.

But still. I don't know how to get from my point A to point B in my head. I hope to remain the superintendent in my district for my entire career. Yet there are still things I hope to do and accomplish even while I'm serving in that role. However, I've learned that I don't need to have all the answers, or be equipped to face every fear before it comes. I just need to be faithful in taking the next best step before me.

WE DON'T NEED TO HAVE ALL THE ANSWERS, OR BE EQUIPPED TO FACE EVERY FEAR BEFORE IT COMES. **WE JUST NEED TO BE FAITHFUL IN TAKING THE NEXT BEST STEP BEFORE US.**

Fear Makes You Stronger

Eleanor Roosevelt once said, "You gain strength, courage, and confidence by every experience in which you really stop to look fear in the face. You are able to say to yourself, 'I lived through this horror. I can take the next thing that comes along.'"[5] I noted above that fear doesn't go away; the same fears I struggled with eight years ago are still there, calling my name. But that doesn't mean that I don't become stronger through them and capable of responding differently over time. I'm still battling those fears, but in a whole new way. I have grown more personally in the past six months than I have in the past six years. And the funny thing is that this growth didn't entail one huge step, but rather one small, bold move after another, after another, after another. To the point where after a recent small, bold move, I asked myself, "Who is this person?" The fear is not gone, but my response to it has changed immensely.

---

5   Eleanor Roosevelt, *You Learn by Living: Eleven Keys for a More Fulfilling Life* (New York: Harper & Row, 1960).

OUR FEAR MAY NOT GO AWAY, BUT OUR RESPONSE TO FEAR CAN CHANGE IMMENSELY.

Conclusion

If we are pushing ourselves in an effort to grow and become better in our work, fear will be an ongoing part of our lives. It is not a "one and done" event like failure. It will always be part of my 5 percent. But it can still teach us valuable lessons *and* make us better learners and leaders. As my friend Rebecca Egger shared with me after reading this chapter, "We will learn to live with our fear one way or another—and one of us will be submissive to the other. The question is, who/which will be in control?"

Success is not a destination, and even if you travel through dark, scary places like failure or fear, sometimes those are the *very* places from which things like greatness, hope, and success are born! When we are bold, when we choose action in the midst of fear and *lead anyway*, that courage is the birth of greatness. We must learn to dance with the fear!

WHEN WE ARE BOLD, WHEN WE CHOOSE ACTION IN THE MIDST OF FEAR, WHEN WE LEAD ANYWAY, **THAT COURAGE IS THE BIRTH OF GREATNESS.**

5 TIPS TO THRIVE

1   Don't wait for the fear to subside. Prepare yourself appropriately and just step out, even in the midst of fear.

2   Take the power away from fear by opening up with someone about your worries. Chances are, you will find encouragement and strength as you recognize you're not alone in your feelings.

3   Instead of letting something ruin your day, decide how much weight it deserves and only give it that.

4   The next time you are confronted with fear, reflect on past fears and how you grew stronger through the actions you took in the midst of them. Let that reinforce your belief and launch your action.

5   Like Dale Carnegie said, "Go out and get busy." Big things don't happen in one fell swoop. Just find your next best step and take it.

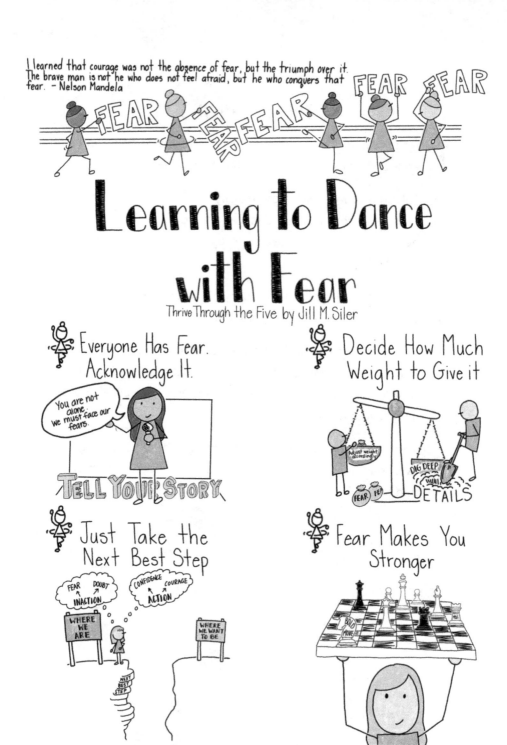

FRAMEWORK TO THRIVE: FEAR

What is one big step you'd like to take personally or professionally?	*What are your fears around taking that step?*
Make social + emotional learning a center point for the library	Executing- I don't Know if "fear" is the right word but I worry that my colleague will "undo" the work because She is harsh

What are the best and worst things that could happen in taking that step?

Best	Worst
Library always appears welcoming Students will feel Safe	Individual will cont. to yell at students or degrade them which will counter efforts

Describe a time when you faced fear head-on. How did your thoughts prior to taking your bold step differ from your thoughts after you did it?

I have addressed this with her but she manipulates the situation by crying —> many teachers have seen her attitude too and don't want to bring their students in w/ her

What is the "next best step" you could take to help move yourself along the path toward where you want to be?

Stay in my lane and do my own thing

On a scale of 1–10, 10 being it is definitely happening, where is your commitment level? What could move that number higher?

7 ish

How does the understanding that fear is a natural part of growing and leading help you think about thriving in the 5 percent?

· Sometimes coming to work is like

THREE

WHEN THE PRESSURE IS HIGH

Successful people do the things
that unsuccessful people
are unwilling to do.

—JOHN MAXWELL

I began swimming my sophomore year of high school in a small town outside of Rochester, New York. I improved a lot that first season and even ended up finishing a surprising third place at our district meet. That summer, I attended a swim camp and spent a week with some great coaches and swimmers. I learned so much and met a group of really nice high school swimmers who were all from East Aurora, a small town outside of Buffalo. The week came to a close, and as I arrived home and unpacked my bags, I found my parents sitting at the kitchen table. They asked me to sit down and began to share the news that my dad had gotten a new job and that we were moving for my junior year of high school . . . to Buffalo. They knew how difficult this was going to be for me but said I could help them decide where to live by helping them choose the school district. I told them I wanted to move to East Aurora, and we did!

That transition was the first time I recall a massive change in expectations. The team at my previous school was good, and the coaches were fantastic, but I was new to swimming and my sudden improvement had occurred toward the end of the season. On the new high school's swim team, it was a whole new world. These girls were fast! (We had three Division I swimmers on our relay when I graduated.) And they trained hard! If I was used to 5x100s freestyle on intervals of 1:45 or 1:40, these girls were going 10x100s free on 1:10! Not a slight difference—that's a massive difference. We ended up winning multiple state titles in our relays together, setting one state record and qualifying for All-American consideration in two different relays. I never could have made the leap to swim at the Division I level without that experience. But I'm not going to lie— the transition to that level of training and competition was incredibly difficult!

I've experienced a similar shift in expectations at different points in my career. Once, when serving as an assistant principal, I told my principal I would be interviewing for an associate principal position in a neighboring district. He smiled and said I should get ready: it was a different place, and I'd need to be on my A game every day. I tend to think that every educator and leader is on their A game every day. But he was right; it was different. Everyone in the system—from students to teachers to parents, central office, and the entire school community—seemed to have greater demands. It was an incredible place to work! But the transition was *hard*.

I have also experienced a shift in expectations when I changed roles. I shared earlier about my apprehensions around moving into the superintendency, and I'll be honest: there were moments in the first two years where I vacillated from looking/feeling like a deer in headlights to actually contemplating getting out. As a campus and central office leader, the demands were high and the challenges difficult, but they were limited to that campus or that role. As a superintendent, you are leading through challenges from every campus, along with managing the budget, handling HR concerns, working with the media, and trying to meet the expectations of seven board members. When you're in that ultimate position where the buck truly stops with you, the expectations couldn't be higher—and neither are the rewards.

Joining new peer groups can also heighten expectations. I had the honor of becoming part of Texas's Future-Ready Superintendent Leadership Network, a group of district leaders who design learning experiences for one another to create more authentic, empowering learning experiences for our students. The first couple of times I heard about the incredible things that these districts were doing, I walked away with my head spinning, thinking, *There's no way I can accomplish all of that with the limited staff in my small district.* The more integrated I became with the group, the more pressure I felt to achieve the "right" work in my district and to know that I was walking the walk, not just talking the talk.

Sometimes our 5 percent comes from a place of pressure or high expectations. We are uncomfortable because expectations have been raised, the pressure is high, and we feel like we're the only ones in this.

PRACTICAL TRUTHS TO POWERFULLY LEAD THROUGH HIGH EXPECTATIONS

Embrace the Goal

If you can come up for air long enough to reflect, you'll realize that there is nothing more powerful than being surrounded by people with high expectations. I had the honor of being part of two incredibly high-performing districts, and there definitely can be such a thing as "winning problems." The first time we went to the state championship in football while I was superintendent, the superintendent of the opposing state semifinalist district pulled my high school principal and me aside to give us tips on managing what was about to happen. He also shared some profound words: that everything was about to change. We didn't realize what he meant until weeks later, but the learning came fast and was difficult at times. Our students, parents, and teachers all began to coalesce around the notion that "nothing was good enough." No program was good enough—even though we were performing at high levels. Once your organization tastes an elite level of success, every part of the organization wants to rise to that level. And, by the way, my school community was right. We had the talent within our students and staff to reach higher levels, but we had not yet done so. It has been absolutely phenomenal—and truly difficult—to lead the entire system as it rose.

ONCE AN ORGANIZATION TASTES AN ELITE LEVEL OF SUCCESS, EVERY PART OF THAT ORGANIZATION **WILL WANT TO RISE TO THAT LEVEL.**

The same is true in our lives and in our work. Once we reach a level of excellence, it is nearly impossible to go back. Author Dr. Henry Cloud noted, "There are certain awakenings that people have—in life and in business—that once they have them, they never go back to the old way of doing things. And when that happens, they are never the same. In short, they got it."[1]

It has been exhilarating to watch and be a part of this in our district, but leading through rising expectations is challenging! The thing to remember is that high expectations make you better—whether they come from a new boss, new colleagues, a new district or organization, or new performance standards. This also relates to the expectations we have for others. Johann Wolfgang von Goethe wrote, "When we treat man as he is, we make him worse than he is; when we treat him as if he already were what he potentially could be, we make him what he should be." The expectations we hold for ourselves and

---

1   Henry Cloud, *Never Go Back: 10 Things You'll Never Do Again* (New York: Howard Books, 2014).

others shape us into who we could and should be. Embrace the high standard, and know that you'll be better for it!

Get After It and Give Yourself Grace

When you find yourself in a situation where expectations are heightened and the pressures are high, you have two choices: sink or swim. (I'm just glad the analogy is not walk or run because you all know I don't do well on land.) If you're reading this book, you're definitely a swimmer—yay!—so cheer yourself on and know that this is a season. Expectations won't lessen, but you will acclimate to those expectations, and in time your day in, day out will not feel like it does right now. Dive in. Learn what you need to learn. Reach out to others. Find a mentor. Develop an action plan for your own growth. Get after it!

But in the same breath, give yourself grace. Understand that the feeling of being overwhelmed, and even at times inadequate, is part of the growing process and not a sign that you're not right for the job or that you lack the skills necessary to be successful in the situation.

> ## UNDERSTAND THAT THE FEELING OF BEING OVERWHELMED, AND EVEN INADEQUATE, IS PART OF THE GROWING PROCESS AND NOT A SIGN THAT YOU'RE NOT THE PERSON FOR THE JOB.

There will be moments when you crush it and others where you wish you would have handled things differently. Through it all, take time to reflect on your own growth. Celebrate the small victories. Cling to the encouragers in your life. Be mindful of staying healthy—both physically and emotionally. Most of all, be thankful for the context that is raising your learning and leadership. Give yourself grace.

Speak the Vision

When expectations are raised, there often is a lot of new growth coming at you (new expectations to meet, new learning from a job change, a paradigm shift from learning from others). One of the greatest strategies of leading through those seasons is to become really clear about your vision—what it is you are trying to do, why you are doing it, how you will do it, and how you want to be throughout it. When you find yourself feeling underwater, come up for air, think about what is most important at that juncture, crystallize your focus around how you need to be leading, and then share that vision with others. Jon Gordon talks about this as the "North Star":

> The vision a positive leader creates and shares serves as a North Star that points and moves everyone in an organization in the right direction. The leader must continually point to this North Star and remind everyone that this is where we are going. Yes, we were here yesterday. Yes, this is what happened in the past. But this is where we are going now. We don't have a perfect set of plans because the world is always changing, but we do have a North Star that will guide us . . . Let's keep our eyes on the North Star and keep moving forward.[2]

Honor the Past and Strive toward the Future

When coming into a new situation or new set of expectations, understand and honor the past, and set a course toward the future. Unless you are starting something completely from scratch, you are walking into something (a district/role/team/etc.) that has a history. A legacy,

---

2   Jon Gordon, "How Leaders Create and Share a Positive Vision," July 17, 2017, http://www.jongordon.com/positivetip/create-and-share-vision.html.

even. While you may not agree with everything that has been done, there is so much good that comes from understanding and valuing the history of all of the work that was put in to bring the organization to that point.

At the same time, we can't live in the past or cling to how things used to be done. Todd Whitthorne, chief inspiration officer of the personal wellness organization Naturally Slim, shares that "the ratio between the rearview mirror and the windshield is telling . . . don't trip over things behind you."[3] Clearly our sights need to be set in front of us. We have to move our organizations (and the people within them) forward. The innovator George Couros says this about this change: "The goal isn't to change for the sake of change but to make changes that allow us to empower our teachers and students to thrive."[4] The same is true in our own lives—the goal isn't change for change's sake. The goal is to look for areas where we can thrive, where we can empower others in our organizations to thrive—and then to support our people in moving toward them.

Conclusion

Sometimes our 5 percent comes from a place of discomfort with our ability to handle our challenges. When expectations are high or changing, know that this is a season and you will grow and acclimate. Be thankful for the context that is raising your learning and leadership. Get after it and give yourself grace!

---

3   Todd Whitthorne is the chief inspiration officer (*Can I have that title?*) of Naturally Slim, a digital counseling program that helps people find success in the area of personal wellness: http://toddwhitthorne.com/. This particular presentation at the TASA Leadership Summit in July 2019 was entitled "Overcoming the Odds."

4   George Couros, *The Innovator's Mindset: Empower Learning, Unleash Talent, and Lead a Culture of Creativity* (San Diego: Dave Burgess Consulting, Inc., 2015).

IN SEASONS WHERE YOU FIND A CHANGE IN EXPECTATIONS, BE THANKFUL FOR THE CONTEXT THAT IS RAISING YOUR LEARNING AND LEADERSHIP.

5 TIPS TO THRIVE

1 When you find yourself under a new level of expectations and pressure, set tangible goals and embrace the season, knowing that it is just a season, as you will acclimate.

2 Consider what could help you grow the most. Is it finding a mentor or colleague who is particularly skilled in an area? Is it reading up on all aspects of the issue? Is it starting out a little earlier to get some of the "work" done so that you can spend the time necessary where the action is during the day?

3 Don't miss an opportunity to speak the vision. Ground yourself and everyone around you in what you're doing and why you're doing what you're doing.

4 Reflect on the legacy of your organization and the people who have contributed to that. Celebrate their work and find ways to incorporate their leadership and learning into the current work.

5 Cling to the encouragers in your life. Be deliberate in spending time with people and work that bring you joy.

Successful people do the things unsuccessful people are unwilling to do.
—John Maxwell

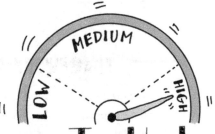

When the Pressure Is High

Thrive Through the Five by Jill M. Siler

Embrace the Goal

High Expectations Make You Better

Get After It & Give Yourself Grace

Feeling overwhelmed?

Inadequate?

"It's part of the growing process!"

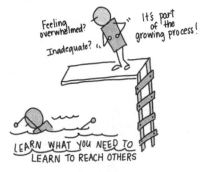

LEARN WHAT YOU NEED TO LEARN TO REACH OTHERS

Speak the Vision

BE CLEAR

WHAT ARE YOU TRYING TO DO?

WHY ARE YOU DOING IT?

HOW WILL YOU DO IT?

WHO DO YOU WANT TO BE THROUGH IT?

Honor the Past & Strive Toward the Future

FUTURE
PAST

The ratio between the rear view mirror and the windshield is telling... don't trip over things behind you

In seasons where you find a change in expectations, be thankful for the context that is raising your learning and leadership.

FRAMEWORK TO THRIVE: PRESSURE

When did you last encounter a season where you felt in over your head?	What strategies did you use to lead through those times?	How long did it take for you to feel like you were in a better place?
The pandmic	• breath • lists • make goals that are tangable	• cuando!

Think about one area of your work or life that is really challenging you . . .

• Working w/ a certain individual that yells, moody, & does not do well with multitasking/ planning

What are three small things you can do to "get after it"?	In what ways do you need to "give yourself grace"?
• patience • talk to ~~the~~ someone in leadership that can offer advise	• outdoor time ○ silence

How does the understanding that high expectations make us better help you think about thriving in the 5 percent?

— ideas ???

PART II

LEADING IN . . .

What are the inward strategies we can employ to help us better lead through the most difficult 5 percent of what we do?

Where does internal self-care connect with our external leadership ability?

How can we leverage our relationships with others, caring for self, understanding that we are enough, and recognizing how and when to make a change in order to thrive through challenging times?

FOUR

LEAD OTHERS AND BE LED

*We make a living by what we get, but
we make a life by what we give.*

—WINSTON CHURCHILL

Years ago, I was working in my office at Central Administration when our deputy superintendent, Dr. Diane Frost, popped into my office and asked me to lunch. Diane and I had worked in the same district for several years, but we were not close friends. We didn't call each other, we didn't serve on cabinet together, we had never gone to lunch with each other by ourselves. She had just been named lone finalist for the superintendent position at Corsicana ISD, and I knew she would be transitioning in a matter of weeks. I eagerly said yes.

After she ordered, Diane began to unpack her bag. She pulled out a notebook, portfolio, folders of papers—the items just kept coming—and she began to spread them across our table. When I looked at her quizzically, she said, "I am going to teach you how to get a superintendent job." I had just finished my doctorate and been promoted from director to executive director, but I had no intentions of becoming a superintendent.

When I expressed this to her, Diane quickly replied, "Yes, you will be" and began walking me through the entire process. She told me how to find the jobs on TexasISD.com, how to establish relationships with search firms, how to lay out a résumé for that kind of position, and how to prepare for the different rounds of interviews.

Diane and I are now close friends, and we have been serving as sister superintendents for the past eight years. When she deliberately took time and energy to help me, I had not asked her to be my mentor; in fact, *I didn't even know that I needed that knowledge or influence in my life.* But she did it anyway.

We've all heard "to whom much is given, much will be required." When it comes to leadership, part of that sacred responsibility is lifting others up along the way. Gandhi noted that "a sign of a good leader is not how many followers you have but how many leaders you create." Leadership expert John Maxwell would also add, "Leading well is not about enriching yourself—it's about empowering others."[1] The work of a truly exceptional leader goes beyond that person. It involves pouring into others *and* ensuring that we have people pouring into us.

Mentors are trusted exemplars or guides, but the actual origin of the word dates back to the end of the eighth century when Homer wrote *The Odyssey*. Mentor was a person, a trusted friend of Odysseus who stayed behind during a war to watch over Odysseus's son. The word was then adapted to mean "someone who teaches or gives help and advice."[2]

I share the word's origin because that imagery of growing up under someone else's guidance, teaching, and coaching is powerful. When looking back on my own journey, I have had *so* many mentors, so many people who have poured into me, and so many I've had the great fortune of growing up under as a leader.

---

1   John Maxwell, *The 21 Irrefutable Laws of Leadership: Follow Them and People Will Follow You* (Nashville: Thomas Nelson, 1998).

2   History Disclosure Team, "Word 'Mentor' Originated from Homer," History Disclosure. Retrieved September 29, 2019, https://www.historydisclosure.com/word-mentor-originates-homer/.

While the relationship between Mentor and Odysseus was unique, it's problematic to think that one single person holds the keys to unlock your future. The chief executive and writer Sheryl Sandberg said:

> I realized that searching for a mentor has become the professional equivalent of waiting for Prince Charming. We all grew up on the fairy tale "Sleeping Beauty," which instructs young women that if they just wait for their prince to arrive, they will be kissed and whisked away on a white horse to live happily ever after. Now young women are told that if they can just find the right mentor, they will be pushed up the ladder and whisked away to the corner office to live happily ever after. Once again, we are teaching women to be too dependent on others.[3]

Finding the keys to the kingdom shouldn't be the goal. The goal is to learn and grow and become a better leader, teacher, and human being. Look at the people in your life and realize who is serving as a mentor for you—whether they know it or not. The question is not "Who is your mentor?" The question is "Who are all of the people in your life who are serving as mentors to you right now?"

FINDING THE KEYS TO THE KINGDOM SHOULDN'T BE THE GOAL. **THE GOAL OF MENTORSHIP IS TO LEARN AND GROW AND BECOME A BETTER LEADER, TEACHER, AND HUMAN BEING.**

---

3   Sheryl Sandberg, *Lean In: Women, Work, and the Will to Lead* (New York: Knopf, 2013).

The Odyssey image of a mentor is much different than that of a role model. There is a marked difference between a role model and a mentor. A *role model* is someone you look up to for a specific reason (their character, their expertise, their talents or abilities). But a *mentor* is someone who counsels you on how to grow your character, expertise, talents, and abilities. We can have mentors in our life around our parenting, our work, our faith, and in countless other areas.

The ideal for mentorship is to be embedded in a personal or professional relationship, but nowadays mentoring can happen without us even knowing that person personally. So many people have reached out to me in this past year sharing that, while I don't know them, I've been a mentor to them. In the same way, I look to leaders and authors like Brené Brown, Jon Gordon, and Jon Acuff, or to extraordinary coaches like Texas A&M's Buzz Williams and others for inspiration, exhortation, and insight.

PRACTICAL TRUTHS TO POWERFULLY LEAD OTHERS AND BE LED

People Are Looking to You

I know what some of you are thinking: *I'm not in that position of leadership that I want to reach, but these are great notes to keep in mind for when I get there.* Umm . . . no. Regardless of the position you are in or aspire to be in, there are people who are looking to *you* for leadership. Lead them.

Even as a first-year teacher, I often found myself working with others on classroom projects. People would pop into my room to see what I was up to. Now, my craft was rough, but my enthusiasm and creativity were powerful. It doesn't matter what your current role is, there are people all around you who are looking to you for counsel and guidance.

REGARDLESS OF THE POSITION YOU ARE IN OR ASPIRE TO BE IN, **THERE ARE PEOPLE WHO ARE LOOKING TO YOU FOR LEADERSHIP. LEAD THEM.**

Pour In

I am deeply passionate about raising up leaders. Right now, I am mentoring several who are aspiring to lead at our central office, another handful who are aspiring to the superintendency, and a few more who are serving in their first year as superintendents. That means a lot of lunches and breakfasts and coffees and 10:00 p.m. phone calls, but it is also incredibly rewarding. Not just for me, but for the students across our state these individuals are serving.

There are so many people who are absolutely capable to lead at the next level but are held back by their lack of confidence. Consequently, when someone discusses their fears as they contemplate a next step and then follows up by sharing the incredible things they've achieved by taking that step of faith, it can be powerful. It can instill a belief in others that they can do it, too.

The people I mentioned above are my "formal" mentoring relationships. But informally, I hope that many people feel I've had a hand in mentoring them—and I can name dozens who mentored me. The ask isn't to go one by one to the people in our circles to see if we can be their mentor or if they can be ours. Our responsibility is to *pour in* to the lives of those around us and *seek out* those leading in incredible ways around us—and to let those relationships find us naturally.

We Need to Be Led

Equally important, we need to make sure that we are being *led*. So often as we rise in our leadership, there are fewer and fewer people to help lead us in our journeys. Sometimes because we have already arrived where we were trying to go, and sometimes because our mentors have turned into colleagues and friends along the way.

As I look back on my leadership journey, my life would have looked *drastically* different had people not poured into me along the way. In fact, I started to make a list of everyone who has impacted me to include here, but thirteen paragraphs later, I realized I could never name them all, nor do my gratitude justice. Some of these folks helped my entry into leadership; some of them taught me lessons in how to run a school, write curriculum, and build systems; and some of them taught me that the work was nowhere near as important as the people.

Sometimes the mentoring happens without our prompting, as with Diane. But sometimes seeking mentoring is absolutely calculated. When I began applying for superintendent positions, I called people I knew and trusted and asked as many questions as I could. When I encounter issues in my work, I always call people who have been there, who can provide experienced counsel. Even as I was starting the process of writing this book, I cold-called multiple authors I respect and asked as many questions as I possibly could. We need to be led, and *we are the drivers of that learning*.

Before becoming a superintendent, I had the opportunity to attend our state's Aspiring Superintendent Academy, where I met one of the facilitators, Dr. Jenny Preston, the former superintendent of Graham and Allen School Districts in Texas. I was so impressed by the confident and graceful way she led (and also decided I wanted to be like her when I grew up). After the academy finished, I asked her if we could meet for coffee, and she said yes! So, I drove to meet her—420 miles round trip. I share this because sometimes being led requires massive effort on our parts. We can't ask someone to mentor us and then vaguely hope it will happen. We must create opportunities and put in the effort to make it happen. If you want to meet with someone to learn from them, you go to them. When we seek mentorship, we need to go the distance (sometimes literally) to make it happen, because it is important.

An interesting side note: I made the final decision to take the leap and apply for a superintendency on a Friday afternoon in early March. The very next Tuesday, the Gunter ISD superintendent position was posted. And the search firm happened to be led by Dr. Jenny Preston, who I had driven seven hours to visit two months earlier. Good things don't happen to those who wait; good things happen to those who get after it and make it happen!

WHEN WE SEEK MENTORSHIP, WE MUST GO THE DISTANCE. WE MUST CREATE OPPORTUNITIES AND PUT IN THE EFFORT TO MAKE IT HAPPEN.

My mentor relationships (those mentoring me) look different today than they did twenty years ago, but they still happen. And they are still as critically important. No matter where we are in our leadership journey, we will not be our best if we don't continue to seek people who challenge us, pour into us, and can see further into us than we can see ourselves. Each of us needs to be leading others, and each of us needs to be led!

It Starts with Me

John Maxwell shared in *Leadership Gold* that even after leading thousands himself, his greatest challenge as a leader was "leading me." He went on to say that:

> Most people use two totally different sets of criteria for judging themselves versus others. We tend to judge others according to their actions. It's very cut-and-dried. However, we judge ourselves by our intentions. Even if we do the wrong thing, if we believe our motives were good, we let ourselves off the hook. And we are often willing to do that over and over before requiring ourselves to change.[4]

Mentorship only happens when: 1) we admit that we don't have all the answers, 2) we admit that we're not where we want to be in a particular area, and 3) we desire to actually do something about it.

Psychologist Carol Dweck wrote, "The view you adopt for yourself profoundly affects the way you lead your life. It can determine whether you become the person you want to be and whether you accomplish the things you value."[5]

We can all grow and change and lead in a different way, but only if we believe we can and then work hard toward achieving that. Part of that is being open to realizing that we're not perfect. Author and speaker Simon Sinek notes that "leadership comes from telling us not what we want to hear, but rather what we need to hear. To be a true leader is to engender deep trust and loyalty, [and it] starts with telling the truth."[6] We need to be seeking truth-tellers in our life so that we can start to tackle the growth.

---

4 John Maxwell, *Leadership Gold: Lessons I've Learned from a Lifetime of Leading* (Nashville, Thomas Nelson, Inc., 2008).

5 Carol Dweck, *Mindset: The New Psychology of Success* (New York: Ballantine Books, 2006).

6 Simon Sinek, *Leaders Eat Last: Why Some Teams Pull Together and Others Don't* (New York: Penguin, 2014).

Mentorship looks different at every season of our lives. There are seasons where we are so thankful that there are people pouring into our lives. And there are seasons where we are blessed by the people we have the opportunity to pour into. But the magic happens when we realize that the pouring can happen both ways at one time. That we can be leading others while being led ourselves.

I am so thankful for my sister superintendents in Texas. Especially when there were not many of us, these first few women were intentional about building relationships and unity with one another and helping each other grow. The superintendency is not very different from corporate America, with women and other traditionally underrepresented populations sharing a small percentage of leadership roles. The difference in education, though, is that "70 percent of teachers and the majority of principals are female."[7] Yet only 23 percent of superintendents are female (an increase from just 12 percent in 1997).

One of the ways I believe Texas has increased this percentage has been through intentional mentoring and networking. Our state organization for female leadership is thriving. The mission of the Texas Council of Women School Executives (TCWSE) is simple: to empower and equip women leaders. From hosting Superintendent Summits to a simple GroupMe chat and Trello board for sitting female superintendents, we share our challenges and our best resources for successful leadership. This is back-and-forth mentorship, one minute pouring in, the next being led ourselves, and all the while being encouraged and inspired—and it is beautiful.

Conclusion

There is no perfect mentor or perfect mentor relationship, but there are people all around us that we can learn from—if we're willing and actually put in the effort. In the same way, we will never be at the highest spot or know as much as we want to know, but there are people

---

7   Emily Donaldson, "A Seat at the Table: Where Are All the Female Superintendents?" Rivard Report, April 1, 2018, https://therivardreport.com/a-seat-at-the-table-where-are-all-the-female-superintendents/.

all around us who could benefit if we would pour into others what we have learned along our journey—or, even better, if we just walk with them and find ways to let them shine. As Simon Sinek notes, "A mentor is not someone who walks ahead of you to show you how they did it. A mentor walks alongside you to show you what you can do."

In order to thrive through the 5 percent, we first need to learn how to survive through the most challenging moments. And the relationships you have with people, those who speak truth into you, who see more in you than you see yourself, who walk alongside you to show you what *you* can do, will help you move from being able to survive to truly thriving.

NO MATTER WHERE WE ARE IN OUR LEADERSHIP JOURNEY, WE WILL NOT BE OUR BEST IF WE DON'T SEEK OUT PEOPLE WHO CHALLENGE US, WHO POUR INTO US, AND WHO CAN SEE FURTHER INTO US THAN WE CAN SEE OURSELVES.

5 TIPS TO THRIVE

1 Find a professional learning opportunity that will challenge you, and make plans to attend. Buy that book you've heard others talk about (or open the one on your nightstand that's been there for a while) and just read ten pages per night.

2 Consider doing a 360-degree profile to get a better assessment of how you see your leadership and how your colleagues see you.

3 Commit to investing in someone. Start small—maybe ask them for coffee. Ask questions about what they love about what they do and what they see in their future. Share the positive traits that you see in them.

4 Ask someone you respect and would like to learn from to lunch. Ask questions about their journey, their greatest hopes, and the challenges they've walked through.

5 Strengthen your professional learning network. When you're at meetings and in professional learning, be intentional about meeting people. Online, follow people you admire or even participate in a Twitter chat.

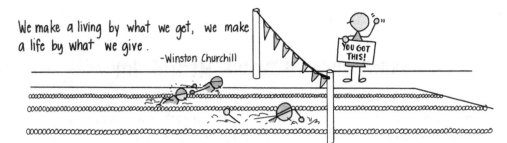

Lead Others & Be Led

Thrive Through the Five by Jill M. Siler

Finding the keys to the kingdom shouldn't
be the goal. The goal is to learn and grow
and become a better leader, teacher,
and human being.

FRAMEWORK TO THRIVE: MENTORSHIP

Who has impacted your life? Name five mentors and the greatest lessons they taught you.	*How are you different today because of the people who have poured into you?*
Who around you is looking to you for leadership? How are you actively mentoring others?	*Who is currently serving as a mentor in your life? Who would you want to learn from that you could actively seek out?*

How does thinking through mentorship in a broader way help you think about thriving in the 5 percent?

FIVE

CARE FOR YOURSELF FIRST

Rest and self-care are so important. When you take time to replenish your spirit, it allows you to serve others from the overflow. You cannot serve from an empty vessel.

—ELEANOR BROWN

We cannot thrive though challenging times ourselves or help others thrive when we are not at our best. We must unapologetically take care of ourselves.

I am a firm believer that you can't walk others down a road you haven't traveled and triumphed yourself. (So, let's be clear that I will not be writing a book about raising teenagers anytime soon!) But this particular chapter is tricky, because I am not sure I have "arrived" yet in terms of mastering balance or practicing self-care. In fact, I am sure that there are some who would look at my life and say that I have absolutely no balance or that my level of balance and my practice of self-care is unacceptable to them.

Even in the crisis of the moment (currently the global coronavirus pandemic, which has forced school closures around the globe), I find that I have placed self-care up on the dusty top shelf, hoping that no one discovers it is not being practiced. In the past several weeks, I have had several opportunities to be interviewed for various podcasts and articles. One of them was Tom Murray's Future Ready Schools national network.[1] He asked question after question about my leadership throughout this crisis, and my responses were spot-on: how as a rural district with little technology, we had shifted to a robust online learning platform in a matter of days; how we aggressively distributed every device we had to students and purchased internet hotspots for every family without internet in our community; how we pooled community resources to deliver groceries to families who were in need throughout the crisis.

My responses were flawless, one after another . . . until he asked how I was taking care of myself. The truth is I've worked almost thirty days straight, I've had more than my fair share of daily Cokes and M&M's, I am struggling to sleep on a nightly basis, and I feel like my entire body has atrophied.

Here's the real truth: When you become the leader, you give up the right to walk out at 4:00 p.m., to not dwell on work-related items after-hours, to sleep easy. And the larger the leadership role, the more "weight" you carry—and that has real impact and costs. But that doesn't mean that you have to place self-care on the dusty shelf. Every day is a new day. This morning I woke up, made French toast for my family, went on a walk with my daughter, and will be home early for family movie night. And tomorrow I will try again.

There are a lot of ideas out there around work-life balance—from mantras around minimal workweeks to encouraging being all-in. What I've come to believe is that there is no easy answer or solution to balance, nor is it something that can be "achieved" and then be done with. Rather, it's a struggle to attain and maintain balance because our life and work circumstances are constantly in flux. It is something I grapple with regularly. And honestly, if I weren't grappling with it regularly, I probably wouldn't be a very good superintendent or a very good mom/wife/daughter/friend, right?

---

1   Thomas C. Murray, "Vulnerability & Mindset with Dr. Jill Siler," May 28, 2020, https://www.youtube.com/watch?v=9W3vMgJOrok&feature=youtu.be.

The last disclaimer I would add is that I think it is difficult for anyone to speak about work-life balance while in the midst of trying to attain it. I am acutely aware that I may look back at my life in twenty years and wish I had lived differently. I hope that's not the case. But I am certainly self-aware enough to know that it is a possibility. Having shared those disclaimers, I will share a few thoughts on how I live this life of being a wife and a mom along with being a superintendent of a stellar school district, an adjunct professor, a frequent speaker, and a writer.

PRACTICAL TRUTHS TO POWERFULLY LEAD BY CARING FOR SELF

Balance Does Not Happen in a Day

I would love to say that every day is balanced—that I wake up and spend an hour by myself, in nature, getting grounded for the day, and then do a vigorous workout, have a deep conversation with my spouse, make breakfast for my kids, walk them to school, have a meaningful day at work, prepare dinner for the family, attend the kids' practices, play a board game before bed, and then read a story together as they blissfully fall asleep. I'm going to be honest: most Mondays do not look like that in my world. Neither do any other days of the week.

While striving for daily balance is great, I assess balance in longer timeframes:

- I know Tuesday is going to be crazy with a 7:00 a.m. education foundation meeting, 4:00 p.m. district advisory meeting, and 6:00 p.m. board meeting, but I also know that I have nothing on my calendar past 4:30 p.m. on Wednesday.
- I know that October, April, and May look like a catastrophic event hit my calendar, but I also know that June, July, November, and December look barren in comparison, at least as far as evenings go.

- I know that I am taking this new position (i.e., when I became superintendent) and that my first six months are going to be crazy (as there is no substitution for visibility and building relationships in a new position), but that those six months are not reflective of what that job will look like two years down the road.
- I know I work year-round and my job is kind of 24/7 in nature, but I also know that as an executive leader, I have six weeks of vacation built into my calendar (a week at Thanksgiving, two at Christmas, one at spring break, and two in the summer), and that is pretty incredible!

Another strategy I use with my calendar is to create a schedule of events. Being in a one-high-school town, I can easily fall into a "I must be at everything" mentality, which is unsustainable. I attend every district home varsity game and all playoff games, and try to hit at least one subvarsity and middle-school event each season. When you add in all of the fine arts events, academic banquets, and other major extracurricular events, the calendar fills up quickly. I create a schedule that reflects support for all programs but is also realistic for my family. It's not perfect, but it's a constant give-and-take.

I love how Tom Knebel, senior associate at the people-development organization GiANT, frames time management: Divert Daily (find some quiet moments every day), Withdraw Weekly (set aside time each weekend for rest and relaxation), Maintain Monthly (structure some personal retreat time every few months), and Abandon Annually (complete respite for a period of time).[2]

Try to keep a thirty-thousand-foot view of balance, and remember that while every day is not going to be perfectly balanced, you can still achieve balance over time.

---

2   Tom Knebel, "There's a Nap for That," January 13, 2015, http://tompnebel.com/theres-a-nap-for-that/.

BALANCE DOES NOT HAPPEN IN A DAY. THE GOAL IS NOT FOR MONDAY TO BE PERFECTLY BALANCED. THE GOAL IS FOR YOUR LIFE TO HAVE A SENSE OF BALANCE.

Balance as Emotional Preoccupation

Balance isn't always about physical location as much as it is emotional preoccupation. Sometimes balance is less about the number of hours spent working and more about the number of hours that you dwell on work-related things. There are many days where I might be physically home and doing "life," but my mind is elsewhere and my stress level is high. Sometimes the remedy is unplugging when you get home; sometimes it is taking a minute to talk the issue through with a colleague so that you know how to approach the issue the next day, and you can finally set it aside for the night. Regardless of the strategy, it is important to realize that we need to be as "all-in" at home as we are at work.

Emotional preoccupation can also occur because we forget our "why." I love Simon Sinek's TED Talk on this subject, in which he says that work isn't about what we do or how we do it—it's about *why* we do it in first place.[3] When we're talking about managing our emotional preoccupation, remembering your *why* is crucial. Jon Gordon adds, "We don't get burned out because of what we do. We get burned out because we forget why we do it."[4] When I am getting overwhelmed, I

---

3   Simon Sinek, "How Great Leaders Inspire Action," TEDxPuget Sound, September 2009, https://www.ted.com/talks/simon_sinek_how_great_leaders_inspire_action?language=en.

4   Jon Gordon, "Know Your Why: What Is Your Purpose?" July 10, 2017, http://www.jongordon.com/positivetip/know-your-why.html.

take a step back to remember why I'm doing what I'm doing. I visit a campus and talk with kids and teachers about the incredible things they are doing, and it centers my thinking and my work around my purpose!

Turn It Off

Part of balance is being intentional about how we work at home. In our lives as leaders, working at home will not always be avoidable. But as I have become more cognizant of this issue, I find myself asking, "Do I absolutely have to do this at this moment?" Balance starts with the leader. It's one thing to send an email that's going to be in the recipient's inbox the next day, versus sending a text that prompts immediate action. Sometimes I email myself reminders to follow up on an issue I need to discuss, but there just isn't that same level of urgency in an email. The bottom line is that the leader drives the culture. If you begin to back off working after-hours, your people will, too. And everyone will be happier.

Part of turning it off is getting out of Dodge. We must find respite and turn off the stresses of life in order to be refreshed. Our family loves to travel, and we do so creatively and inexpensively. We take road trips, pack groceries, stay in our timeshare, etc. And that time is a game changer. It removes us from our house, our work, our busy lives (and sometimes even our cell phones) when we need it the most. We hike. We swim. We watch movies. We play games. We spend time together. As leaders, sometimes we need to step away to better see how to move ourselves and our districts forward.

While taking time off is critical and vacation is one of my favorite parts of life, it's not enough. My family has really given me a hard time because while writing this book, I often came back from church with a list of ideas that would come to me during the message on Sunday morning. They said I am "off-task" during the message. (I tend to think I was divinely inspired! This is an ongoing argument in the Siler household.)

PART OF FINDING BALANCE IS TAKING RESPITE. AS LEADERS, SOMETIMES WE NEED TO STEP AWAY TO BETTER SEE HOW TO MOVE OURSELVES AND OUR ORGANIZATIONS FORWARD.

Maybe it *is* that—divine inspiration. I'd certainly love to think so! I'd love to think that this book will reach people on a deeper level, not just about what they want to accomplish but about *who* they want to be as human beings. But I also think that part of the inspiration is simply because I stop.

I stop.

And sit.

And listen.

And open my heart and my mind.

And the ideas begin to flow.

Sometimes I write just a few bullet points or lines. And sometimes I write paragraph after paragraph in my smallest handwriting. Sunday mornings have become an inspiration for me, to the point where if I'm having trouble knowing exactly which direction to go next, I tell myself to just hold on until Sunday.

But it's not enough just to wait until Sunday. If we are truly going to be the leaders we aspire to be, we need to make daily time to stop and listen and open our hearts and minds to reflect on where we are and where we want to be, and on who we are and who we want to be.

"Turning it off" is not just about our personal time and space, either. One of the most influential mentors for me as a superintendent has been Dr. Kevin Brown, currently the executive director of TASA, our state's educational leadership organization. As the former superintendent of Alamo Heights, Kevin was renowned for the masterful way he used his calendar. A student of the Breakthrough Coach,[5] an organization whose passion is to build better schools and create more balanced lives, he lived by the mantra "Does your calendar reflect the leader you aspire to be?" He talked about how, in his work as a district leader, he intentionally scheduled the critical work that would move his organization forward on his calendar, including time on his campuses to coach principals along with blocks of time to think, plan, and vision around the biggest levers.

WE CAN'T WAIT TIL SUNDAY. WE NEED TO MAKE TIME TO OPEN OUR HEARTS AND REFLECT EVERY SINGLE DAY.

How often do we go about our day unconsciously going after the low-hanging fruit (email, the issues in front of us, etc.), regardless of their importance, instead of intentionally setting aside time to think, reflect, vision, and plan? How often do we "turn off" all of the other stuff so that we can focus on the critical issues at hand? We need to be intentional with the time we dedicate to our hearts and minds.

Turning it off also means finding things to take my mind off work. We have to have outlets to channel stress. There are so many things we can do to keep our minds (and lives) balanced. I still swim or walk three days a week, and it is critical for my sanity. I love to read, write, hang with the kids, play guitar, and watch movies . . . What exactly you do doesn't matter; just ensure you have an outlet to work through the stress that inevitably comes with the job.

---

5   www.the-breakthrough-coach.com

Make Your Yeses Count

We must learn to say no to make our yeses count. In his influential book, *The 7 Habits of Highly Effective People*, Stephen Covey noted that:

> You have to decide what your highest priorities are and have the courage—pleasantly, smilingly, non-apologetically, to say "no" to other things. And the way you do that is by having a bigger "yes" burning inside. The enemy of the "best" is often the "good."[6]

This is so important (and something I need to improve in)! We must learn how to say no to some things to make room for the things we want to say yes to. As the leader and writer Joelle Jay writes in her book on personal leadership: "The real trick isn't to figure out how to become a master juggler, but to realize that you can only gracefully manage so much before your life feels like a circus."[7]

I have had seasons in my life where I volunteered at church and seasons where I haven't. I've had years where I've volunteered for specific charity organizations and years where I haven't. I've said yes to certain speaking engagements and no to others. Lisa Sugar, the cofounder of POPSUGAR, says this about balance: "You have to balance your passions, not your time."[8]

First Things First

Put your family first. This is critical. My family and I regularly talk about our schedules. When they know that this week/month will be particularly busy but that there are easier weeks/months ahead, it helps.

---

6   Stephen R. Covey, *The 7 Habits of Highly Effective People* (New York: Simon & Schuster, 2013).

7   Joelle Jay, *The Inner Edge: The 10 Practices of Personal Leadership* (Santa Barbara, Praeger, 2009).

8   Lisa Sugar, quoted by Rachel Dresdale in "What Are 'Slash' Careers and Why You Need One," *Forbes*, July 27, 2017, https://www.forbes.com/sites/rachelritlop/2017/07/27what-are-slash-careers-why-you-need-one/#49a5addf3bf6.

I also bring them into my decision-making. When I was asked to speak at a conference in Houston last year during an already crazy time, I presented our spring calendar to my family at dinner, and we talked about whether we could make it work and how we felt about it. I was really leaning toward turning down the opportunity. I shared the very busy-looking calendar with my family, and they disagreed. They said I needed to do it and even offered suggestions on how we could make it work given the other things they had going on that weekend. As it turns out, that speech was one of the turning points of my life. It was the very talk I described in chapter 1 of this book. Had I relied on what I thought they'd say, I would have missed it. Giving our loved ones a voice in how/when we lead can be powerful.

It is also important to put yourself first by giving yourself grace. As school leaders, we're accustomed to long hours and hard work. When I need to take some time here or there, I do it and I don't stress over it. Sometimes that means taking an extra thirty minutes at lunch on a day where I know I have meetings and events that will run into the evening so I can start the dishes and run a load of laundry before leaving the house. Sometimes that means creating a schedule where I am supporting students at their events but not feeling like I have to be physically present for every moment of every event.

Part of keeping your own self in the forefront is making moves that make sense for you at various points in your life. I mentioned that I am sure some people would look at my life and feel that there isn't balance. How could a young mom of two young kids (at the time) go and become a superintendent? Whereas I looked at that juncture in my life this way: God has blessed me with these incredible gifts of leadership and a love for kids and working with teachers and leaders. How can I make a move that makes sense and that allows me to put these gifts to use for others? For me, part of finding balance as a young mom was becoming a superintendent of a small district instead of a large district. Sometimes balance isn't about whether or not you can or should do the job; it's about finding the right job in the context that will work for your family.

SOMETIMES BALANCE ISN'T ABOUT WHETHER OR NOT YOU CAN OR SHOULD DO THE JOB. SOMETIMES IT IS ABOUT **FINDING THE RIGHT JOB IN THE CONTEXT THAT WILL WORK WITH YOUR LIFE.**

Building a support network is critical in life. If I didn't have a strong support network, I couldn't do this work. My husband works long hours, but we share responsibilities with our kids and around the house. My parents were willing to relocate to our area, and that has been a huge blessing for us as well, especially when the kids were young. I also have close friends I call on when I need help with transporting or keeping kids.

One of the things I love the most about working in my school district is that the district (and the community) truly cares about my well-being and the well-being of my family. That is priceless. Therefore, my charge is also to care for the well-being and balance of the people I work with. But be sure that you are in an organization that cares about *you* and your work-life balance.

At the end of the day, I always worry that I will have regrets about how I lived my life. (I am sure we all have these worries.) As Bob Goff would say, "I used to be afraid of failing at something that really mattered . . . Now I'm more afraid of succeeding at things that don't matter."[9] What we do and how we balance our lives matters. But I also know that my family is super proud of me. My family is my first priority, and we cherish our time together every day. And we *love* the weeks we spend together when we're off. It may not be a perfect life,

---

9   Bob Goff, *Love Does: Discover a Secretly Incredible Life in an Ordinary World* (Nashville, Thomas Nelson, 2012).

but it is our life, and it is full of love, meaningful work, and incredible memories—with many more to come!

Conclusion

As you reflect on these thoughts, I'd encourage you to consider areas where you could grow (I have plenty!), but also give yourself some grace and realize that the reason you are plagued with doubts about whether you are balancing your life well is because you care so deeply about those you serve and love—in your work and in life! Part of thriving through the 5 percent of really difficult days and seasons is ensuring that you are well in every aspect of your life (physical, emotional, spiritual), so don't put yourself last. Care for yourself first!

WHEN IT COMES TO BALANCE, GIVE YOURSELF GRACE. REALIZE THAT THE REASON YOU ARE PLAGUED WITH DOUBTS ABOUT WHETHER YOU ARE BALANCING WELL IS BECAUSE YOU CARE SO DEEPLY ABOUT THOSE YOU SERVE AND LOVE.

5 TIPS TO THRIVE

1 Be intentional about your calendar. Look at all the events you could attend this month, and find a balanced way to show support for your work that allows time for your family.

2 When you're facing a really busy week, or couple of weeks, print out your calendar and start a conversation with your family. Share why things are busy and when you'll be freer. Ask for their input on how to make the busy times better for the family.

3 Take up the phones (including yours). The next time you have some great family time planned, put everyone's phone in a box, disconnect with the world, and reconnect with one another. Start with an hour or two and build from there.

4 Set aside time each day to stop. Clear your mind, breathe deep breaths, and reflect on who you are and how you want to be. Maybe put a pen in your hand and jot down your thoughts, your current struggles, or your aspirations. Open your heart and mind.

5 Change your automatic yes to "That sounds incredible; let me think on that possibility." And then weigh the impact of the opportunity with the consequences of what you will not be able to do in light of it. Say no with grace when appropriate.

Care for Yourself First

The real trick isn't to figure out how to become a master juggler, but to realize that you can only gracefully manage so much before your life feels like a circus.

—Joelle Jay

Thrive Through the Five by Jill M. Siler

Balance Does Not Happen in a Day

a sense of balance

BALANCE

Balance as Emotional Preoccupation

hours you work + hours you dwell on work

FOR NOW   FOR LATER

Turn It Off

BE INTENTIONAL ABOUT HOW WE WORK AT HOME

step and sit and listen

Make Your Yeses Count

save for highest priorities

YES   NO

First Things First

GIVE YOURSELF GRACE

BALANCE SCHEDULES

FINDING THE RIGHT JOB

BUILD A SUPPORT NETWORK

FIND AREAS OF GROWTH

family first

If we are truly going to be the leaders we aspire to be, we need to make daily time to stop and listen and open our hearts and minds to reflect on where we are and where we want to be, on who we are and who we want to be.

sketchnote by Amelia Buchanan
@edtech_amelia

FRAMEWORK TO THRIVE: SELF-CARE

In the work you do, what are your busier seasons/months/days?	*In the work you do, what are your less busy seasons/months/days?*
What strategies do you use to "turn it off" at home?	*What strategies are most effective in helping you keep your life in balance?*

What do you currently need to say no to so that you can put your yes on the table for something different?

How does understanding the importance of self-care help you think about thriving in the 5 percent?

S I X

T.P.W.

Anyone can be tough for a season. It takes a special kind of human to rise to life's challenges for a lifetime.

—CHRIS MATAKAS

I didn't start swimming until I was a sophomore in high school. But I knew in the first twelve months that I wanted to go all the way.

Swim in college.

Get a scholarship.

Swim at the Division I level.

There was just one problem. Even though I had these big dreams, I wasn't fast enough to achieve any of them.

When I applied to college, it was back when correspondence came from handwritten notes and applications were completed with a typewriter (though if you were really well-off, you had access to a word processor). Finding colleges consisted of looking at catalogs that came in the mail or visiting your high school counseling office, where there were racks upon racks of college catalogs. To communicate with college coaches, you wrote letters back and forth. And letters I wrote. I made a list of all of the Division I schools in the Northeast that I wanted to attend. I had pretty big dreams academically, too, and so I wrote to the coaches of all of the big schools. The response was either radio silence, swift letters of denial because I was not fast enough, or my favorite, a handwritten note to let me know that there was no way I could swim Division I and that I should set my sights lower. And they weren't wrong. I was a Division III-caliber swimmer attempting to swim at a Division I school.

My response was simple. Just keep swimming. Do the work necessary in the moment to achieve the dream, without knowing if it would be possible to achieve in the end. I began to visit schools my senior year, and those visits reflected both my current reality (Division II and III schools) and my ultimate goal (Division I schools).

One of the Division III schools I visited was a swimming powerhouse: a DIII NCAA Champion for many years. The recruiting trip had every enticement you could imagine—personal touches, a tour of the most beautiful places on campus, being paired with the best swimmers on the team. At the end of every recruiting weekend, the head coach sat recruits down and talked through their future plans with the team and what that would mean, both in terms of their role as a swimmer and in terms of financial support. In his meeting with me, the coach pulled up the top 10 finishes at the prior year's Division III championship, showing me that I would already be in the top 5. I silently thought to myself, *My vision is larger than your vision.* I managed to share in a barely audible voice that my real goal was to make the Olympic Trials cut. And he pulled that sheet out, too, showing me how far off I was, as if to say, "You'll never achieve that."

It was devastating to my seventeen-year-old self.

But I had just one response: Just keep swimming.

I had one high school coach who had gone on to be a graduate assistant at the University of Pittsburgh. She had only seen me swim my very first year, as a sophomore, and knew that I was brand-new to the sport, was over six feet tall, and in the course of four months had managed to finish in the top three in my district. She told her coach about me and pleaded a strong case for them to bring me in. One day I got the phone call to come on a recruiting trip to the Division I University of Pittsburgh.

I flew on a plane by myself, had a driver waiting for me at the airport, and took the long and windy road through the Allegheny Mountains toward the city.

We entered into the Fort Pitt Tunnel, which is literally under Mount Washington. Driving toward it there is zero evidence you are approaching a city, except perhaps for the number of cars on the roadway. The entrance looks like you are in the middle of a forest, about to head through the belly of a mountain. When you get to the other side, however, the three rivers unfold before you, and you see for the first time the mesmerizing city landscape of downtown Pittsburgh.

I had an amazing time on this recruiting trip. I could tell immediately that *this* was a group I would be challenged by, that could help me reach my goals. On the last day, I had my meeting with the coach. He shared with me his excitement that I was considering Pitt, but was also honest that I was not even good enough to be a walk-on for the team. He stated that he believed in me and my coach's assessment of me, though, and was willing to give me a small scholarship that could grow over my time in college as I got faster. I thanked him but also wondered how my family could manage tuition. The other schools I was visiting were offering much more financial assistance. But as I considered my options, my action was the same: just keep swimming.

The spring of my senior year, I didn't make the cuts for the junior national meet, let alone the cuts for senior nationals. So, I ended up going to the regional zone meet. It was at Princeton University, and that was exciting, but I was still disappointed that my swimmer friends were headed to juniors and I was headed to zones. I was swimming with coaches I had never met, in a pool I hadn't swum in before. At the end of the warm-up sprints, the coach began to confer with another coach on deck, who called me over. "What did you say your best time was again?" I told him, and he shook his head and responded, "Your time is going to be a lot faster this weekend." And he was right.

Every single race I swam that weekend was golden. In a sport where you are working to reduce your time by tenths or even hundredths of a second, I was dropping entire seconds in every race I swam. I qualified for junior nationals in every event and overnight became a top recruit in the country.

I returned home and the funniest thing happened: my phone began to ring with offers from every Division I coach who had turned me down, including the one who'd written saying I was crazy for even considering it. I graciously thanked them and turned them all down. And I picked up the phone and called the University of Pittsburgh to let them know I was officially committing to their school. They took a chance on me, and now it was my turn to take a chance on them.

It wasn't that my talent level changed or that the standards at Division I schools changed. I continued to work until my outcomes changed.

YOUR TALENT MAY NOT CHANGE. THE STANDARD MAY NOT CHANGE. BUT YOUR OUTCOME CAN ALWAYS CHANGE WHEN YOU DO THE WORK.

Shifting back to current times, as I was in the final stages of writing this book, I was having a particularly tough day. The kind of day that makes you question your profession. One of my favorite new author friends is Tara Martin, and in her book *Be Real* she talks about the need for us to be relatable and vulnerable with others.[1] And so, let me just be real with you: There are days that I do think about doing *anything* but what I'm doing. This one day was particularly challenging because my problem felt personal. It had to do with feeling hurt by people I loved in my school community. That's what happens when you stay in a place for a long time: relationships grow deeper, which makes everything sweeter, but it also means you can get hurt more deeply. I walked into my office after a difficult conversation, breathed a heavy sigh, and leaned back in my chair. I noticed a magazine on my desk with a letter inside. It was an early copy of my first nationally published article. The topic was, of course, thriving through the most difficult times. I laughed and thought with very real candor, *I am such a fraud*. Here I am publishing articles about thriving through the difficult times when I really just want to find a rock and crawl under it for a few days.

I called a trusted friend who I knew had also faced difficult circumstances, and she shared her brutal story of how difficult things became for her, to the point where the board voted to not renew her contract as superintendent. She went to church that Sunday, and a lady followed her out when the service was over and said, "I'm so sorry that this has happened. What are you going to do now that you just lost your job?" And my friend responded with such grace, "I'm going to work. Just like I did yesterday. And just like I will tomorrow. Because our students are worth it." She reminded me that sometimes, even in the darkest of days, the absolute best thing you can do is just to go back to work. Many years later and that friend is an extremely successful superintendent—in that very district. Just. Keep. Swimming.

If you know about the Gunter Tigers, you know they are a powerhouse in a lot of things. They have been to the state championships in everything from baseball to FFA to girls' basketball to, most recently, football. If you know anything else about the Gunter Tigers,

---

1   Tara Martin, *Be Real: Educate from the Heart* (San Diego, Dave Burgess Consulting, Inc, 2018).

you also know that we always overplay our potential. We might not win warm-up, but we almost always win the game.

In case you've never heard the phrase "we never win warm-up," it refers to that moment when both teams come onto the court or field to warm up. The spectators look at both teams and begin to size up who is going to win. Which athletes are bigger? Which have more agility and speed? To compound this assessment, our football boys are known to warm up in the shell they wear under their pads. And inevitably, the other team warms up in full pads. However, I don't think many people judge us on warm-up any more. After all, we are 60–3 in just the last four years.

The football team has a mantra, and it is "TPW: tough people win." We will always outwork and outprepare an opponent.

A lot of athletic teams have mantras and slogans, but rarely do they emanate throughout an entire organization like this one has ours. One day when my kids were little, we stopped at a frozen yogurt shop, one of those places where you make your own bowl and put your own toppings on. We all made our own bowl and met up at the register. I looked at my nine-year-old daughter's bowl, heaped with every topping imaginable, from Oreo cookies to M&M's to gummy worms to whipped cream and all of the sauces. I laughed and said, "You are going to get sick." She responded, "No, Mom. I have already told my stomach: 'TPW. Just suck it up.'" I laughed, but it made me realize how deeply entrenched this philosophy was for all of our students. Tough. People. Win.

Sometimes when we face difficult circumstances, there is no easy way out. There is no sequence of plans or meetings that we can implement to make a situation go away. But that doesn't mean that you give up. That means that you keep on doing what you need to do to make the situation better. You keep fighting for kids. Sometimes the best thing we can do is just put our head down and go back to work.

PRACTICAL TRUTHS TO POWERFULLY LEAD WHEN YOU NEED TO TOUGH IT OUT

Toughness Is Both How We Think and How We Act

When we think about mental toughness, often our thoughts center around emotion—we need to have thick skin or let a negative comment roll off our back. A group of researchers looked at the idea of "mental toughness" and found that it is a mix of characteristics and traits. In particular, "participants who exhibited high conscientiousness (e.g., those who spend a lot of time preparing and pay great attention to detail) and high extraversion were most likely to score high on mental toughness."[2] The study also linked high scores in mental toughness to ambition. Mental toughness isn't just a feeling; it is a state of mind built over time through our intentional actions of preparation and relentlessly going after our dreams.

Grit Is Essential and Can Grow

Psychologist and author Angela Duckworth describes *grit* as the "passion and perseverance for very long-term goals," "having stamina," and "working really hard to make that future a reality."[3] The beautiful thing is that talent—which is not distributed equally—does not equate to grit, which is ultimately the characteristic that will lead to success.[4] The question then is, how do you grow your grittiness?

---

2   Mark Travers, "How to Tell If You Are Mentally Tough," *Forbes*, August 20, 2019, https://www.forbes.com/sites/traversmark/2019/08/20/how-to-tell-if -you-are-mentally-tough/#16dc3f0a1099.

3   Angela Duckworth's seminal TED Talk, "Grit: The Power of Passion and Perseverance," can be found here: https://www.ted.com/talks/angela_lee _duckworth_grit_the_power_of_passion_and_perseverance?language=en.

4   Angela Duckworth's website has a Grit Scale that you can take to determine how "gritty" you are: https://angeladuckworth.com/grit-scale.

Author Eric Barker[5] had a conversation with Duckworth and shared these ways to grow grit:

1. **Find Your Passion.** The interesting piece here is that Duckworth mentions that "often interest precedes the development of talent." Don't let your current abilities, or lack thereof, narrow your dreams.

2. **Practice and Practice Some More.** You've heard the saying that "practice doesn't make perfect. Perfect practice makes perfect."[6] Duckworth would agree and add that practice needs to be deliberate and especially focused on areas of weakness.

3. **Find Purpose.** Duckworth notes that "interest without purpose is nearly impossible to sustain for a lifetime." Barker sums it up like this: "Gritty people don't merely have a 'job.' They have a *calling* in life."

4. **Have Hope.** Not a fluffy hope of wishes, but a resolved hope of initiative. Two ways the authors recommend building this hope is through a growth mindset, where you believe you can and will improve, and through positive self-talk.

5. **Join a Gritty Group**. When you surround yourself with people who are bold and going after big dreams, there will be pressure to do the same.[7]

As I shared in the opening of this chapter, sometimes our dreams outpace our current abilities. That's not the time to give up; that's the time to dig in! Toughness comes when we exhibit grit and go after what we really want. And we don't stop until we get it.

---

5   Eric Barker is the author of *Barking Up the Wrong Tree: The Surprising Science Behind Why Everything You Know About Success Is (Mostly) Wrong* (New York: HarperOne, 2017).

6   Often attributed to Vince Lombardi, longtime coach of the Green Bay Packers.

7   Erik Barker, "5 Research-Backed Ways to Increase Grit," The Week, May 2016, https://theweek.com/articles/624204/5-researchbacked-ways-increase-grit.

SOMETIMES YOUR DREAMS OUTPACE YOUR CURRENT ABILITIES. **DON'T LOSE SIGHT OF YOUR DREAMS.** WORK AS IF YOU WERE ACHIEVING THEM UNTIL YOU ACTUALLY DO.

Build Resiliency

While grit is having the passion and perseverance to achieve long-term goals, resiliency is the ability to bounce back after failure even stronger than you were before you failed. In 2001, two University of California at Berkeley alumni founded what is now known as the Greater Good Science Center. Their mission is to study "the psychology, sociology, and neuroscience of well-being, and teach skills that foster a thriving, resilient, and compassionate society."[8] Their work centers on ground-breaking scientific research around social and emotional well-being and then how to apply that science to our everyday lives. Their magazine published an article around how to build resilience. One of the main strategies discussed was the need to change the narrative. Kira Newman shares:

> When something bad happens, we often relive the event over and over in our heads, rehashing the pain. This process is called rumination; it's like a cognitive spinning of the wheels, and it doesn't move us forward toward healing and growth.[9]

---

8   Greater Good Science Center, University of California at Berkeley: https://ggsc. berkeley.edu/who_we_are/about.

9   Kira Newman, "Five Science-Backed Strategies to Build Resilience," Greater Good Science Center, November 9, 2016, https://greatergood. berkeley.edu/article/item/five_science_backed_strategies_to_build_resilience.

Interestingly enough, Newman shares that one way to change the narrative is through expressive writing, a process where you write about your feelings to get to the core of the issue at hand. The science shows that people are happier and emotionally healthier when they employ this process. Newman notes that "we're forced to confront ideas one by one and give them structure, which may lead to new perspectives. We're actually crafting our own life narrative and gaining a sense of control."

I can absolutely attest to the power of this practice. I was sharing with my husband that a number of people have asked how I have time or energy to write a book and asked him this simple question: "What have you noticed about me over the last six months?" His response: "Hands down. Happiest you have ever been." And he is right. Part of it is that I have so much personal and professional fulfillment outside of my work that I'm able to leave work at work (as I mentioned in the chapter on self-care, I'm not dwelling on the stress like I used to). And part of it is that the act of writing is cathartic and leads to less stress, greater self-reflection, and better decision-making.

The other strategies to build resilience that Newman shares from the research include facing your fears, practicing self-compassion (a practice she describes as "confronting our own suffering with an attitude of warmth and kindness, without judgment"), meditation, and cultivating forgiveness.

IT IS UNFAIR TO HOPE THAT PERSONAL AND PROFESSIONAL FULFILLMENT WILL COME SOLELY FROM YOUR JOB. CULTIVATE MEANINGFUL PASSIONS IN YOUR LIFE.

How We Talk to Ourselves Matters

This point makes me chuckle a little. After all, this section is on "mental toughness," and I'm writing about positive self-talk—which to some may seem a little fluffy and not very tough. But it is so important! I heard someone say once that they would *never* allow someone to talk to them the way they talk to themselves. Gandhi is renowned for saying, "I will not let anyone walk through my mind with their dirty feet." Yet sometimes we traipse through mud and manure and come right into our own minds without even taking our boots off. How we talk to ourselves matters.

Author Jon Gordon has talked to the best coaches, players, CEOs, and leaders in our country. And when he was asked what the best advice he ever heard was, he said it came from Dr. James Gills, a man who completed the unbelievable feat of a double triathlon six times in his fifties. "I've learned to talk to myself instead of listen to myself," he said.[10] Our thoughts inherently come from a place of doubt—because if we haven't been there yet, there is no direct path to get there. Yet when we place the doubts and negative self-talk aside and begin to speak life and hope and confidence into our dreams, we can build our mental toughness and find success.

Conclusion

The word *thrive* derives from a North Germanic language, Old Norse, spoken in Scandinavia in the ninth through the thirteenth centuries. The word *thrifask* meant "to grasp for oneself."[11] Nowadays, *thrive* is defined in the following ways:

- to grow or develop well or vigorously; to prosper; to flourish[12]

---

10 Jon Gordon, "The Best Advice I've Ever Heard," http://jongordon.com/blog/best-advice-ive-ever-heard/.

11 https://www.collinsdictionary.com/us/dictionary/english/thrive

12 https://www.lexico.com/en/definition/thrive

- to become very successful, happy, or healthy[13]
- to progress toward or realize a goal despite or because of circumstances[14]

Every single one of these definitions is an active verb. *Thriving doesn't just happen.* It is a result of intentional action, growth, development, and progress. *Thriving is also more than just surviving. Thrive* doesn't just mean "to get by," "to make it," or "to maintain." *Thrive* means to prosper, to flourish, and to develop well or vigorously. And lastly, *thriving is exceedingly positive.* The specific words that teach us that are *successful, happy, or healthy*, and *realize a goal*.

A huge part of setting the stage for thriving to occur is our ability to be tough: even when our abilities aren't equal to our dreams, even when faced with seemingly insurmountable obstacles, even when our deepest thoughts doubt our audacious goals. Tough. People. Win. And we can all learn to be tough!

WHEN YOUR DREAMS OUTPACE YOUR ABILITIES, WHEN YOU FACE INSURMOUNTABLE OBSTACLES, WHEN YOU DOUBT YOUR AUDACIOUS GOALS—DIG IN AND GET TO WORK.

---

13 https://www.macmillandictionary.com/us/dictionary/american/thrive

14 https://www.merriam-webster.com/dictionary/thrive

5 TIPS TO THRIVE

1 Talk to yourself this week. Intentionally. Positively. The next time you hear your self-doubt start to pipe up, audibly speak truth into your soul about what you know to be true and the impact that your greatest hopes and dreams will have on the world around you.

2 For your next major event, lesson, or meeting, go the extra mile in preparation. Focus on the little things. How do you want people to feel? How will you transition? How will you close the time and launch people to be great? After the event, reflect on the impact of your specific preparation.

3 When you come across a challenge, consider putting it in writing—not to publish it, or even to share it, but to see if the process helps you position your thoughts in a way that empowers you to lead through the issue with clarity.

4 Ground yourself in hope. When you find yourself resorting back to the "worst possible scenario," flip it to the "best possible scenario." Reflect on the successes won, relationships built, and those around you who believe in you.

5 Think about what "toughing it out" means for you. Is it having the tough conversation instead of lamenting over it? Is it finishing the tedious task instead of dreading it? Whatever "it" is, just do it.

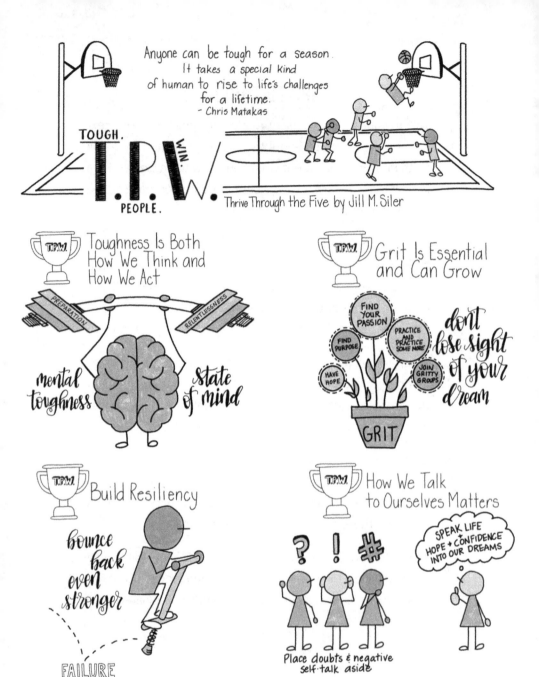

FRAMEWORK TO THRIVE: TOUGH PEOPLE WIN

Describe a time when you "just kept swimming" through tough times.	*As you reflect on that season of your life, what did you learn about yourself?*
Which of the "Five Ways to Grow Grit" do you feel could really move your grittiness forward?	*How are you actively building resilience in your leadership and life?*

How does the understanding that sometimes you just need to tough out the hard times help you think about thriving in the 5 percent?

SEVEN

YOU ARE ENOUGH

You alone are enough.

—OPRAH WINFREY

Writing has opened up so many opportunities for me. Some perhaps expected, and some a total surprise. Writing is a solitary act. It is me and a keyboard. My thoughts. My questions. And the doubts. Is what I'm saying worthwhile? Will anyone be offended or think that I'm talking about a specific situation? Will people think less of me as a leader if I share this particular struggle? I write. I revise. I write some more. And at some point, I finally gain enough courage to hit Publish.

The surprise comes *after* the solitary act of writing, when I hear from the people on the other end. Like when I was stopped while running errands in a nearby town by someone who knew me—not because I was superintendent of the neighboring town, but because of what I have been sharing on Twitter. Or the person who introduced themselves to me at a workshop to thank me for being so vulnerable in my writing. Or the personal notes I have received from people whose lives have been touched by my words. Each time I am surprised and incredibly humbled that my words have impact. And every time

I remember: all of our words have the potential for impact. It is just a matter of whether or not we have the courage to say them.

OUR WORDS HAVE IMPACT. IT IS JUST A MATTER OF WHETHER WE HAVE THE COURAGE TO SAY THEM.

It has been a gift to engage with readers and a privilege to encourage them to take their next best step. That also has meant being online more often than my previous norm. I found myself bombarded with data in this new online world: how many followers I have; how many readers I have; how well the various platforms are engaging with readers; how many likes, retweets, and impressions there are for each post. The list goes on.

And it is difficult to not care about those numbers. Realistically, those numbers matter when you're trying to get published. But the human side tries to take over and compare, contrast, overanalyze, and then doubt. And that leads to tempting, futile thoughts like, *If I could only get _____ amount of followers/readers/etc., I'd be satisfied.* As. If.

It will never be enough. Never. Because once we reach one level, we'll immediately strive for the next. That is human nature. I am learning this in a very visceral way on social media at the age of forty-five for the first time. My daughter, who is just fourteen, already knows this. She lives this. And that is the plight of so many of our young people, who have grown up in a social-media-filled world. Where our days were defined by anecdotal collections of who we were friends with, who we thought got together over the weekend, and maybe even how many notes we passed during the school day, they measure their lives by how many friends and followers they have on each of their social media platforms, how often their phones light up, which publicly shared social gatherings they were part of—and which ones they were not.

One of my favorite leaders out there is a basketball coach named Buzz Williams, whose brave and bold style of leadership has moved teams toward greatness in astounding ways. He shared a video online about his "one word" for this year and I clicked, excited to hear his thoughts.

You can imagine my surprise when his word was *dead*. Williams went on to talk about how this world is nonstop in its chatter. Whether it is mainstream media, social media, or the human beings around us, everyone has an opinion. We no longer question whether it's appropriate to share—it's already public before we really think about it. As Williams said,

> I've spent too much time paying attention to the opinion of others . . . I want to be dead to Twitter's opinion of Virginia Tech basketball . . . I want to be dead to comparing myself to other people. I want to be dead to the noise around me that gets into my head and gets into my soul and messes me up . . . I want to be dead to the things that don't help us.[1]

There are many incredible benefits to our online communities. I have grown and made more bold moves personally in the last six months than I have in the last six years—I owe much of that to literally seeing people in my Professional Learning Network (PLN) doing the work. But we must find a way to engage with the world without becoming fixated on, overtaken by, overwhelmed by, and even obsessed with how that world receives us. And we need to teach our kids to do the same.

---

1 Buzz Williams sharing with his Virginia Tech basketball team his One Word for 2019, https://twitter.com/teamcoachbuzz/status/1085893817675350020. For more on Jon Gordon's powerful One Word movement, visit https://jongordon. com/books/one-word/.

WE HAVE TO FIND A WAY TO ENGAGE WITH THE WORLD BUT NOT BE OVERTAKEN BY HOW THAT WORLD RECEIVES US.

Our worth as human beings is inherent. Our job is to love others and pour into the people around us, knowing that we cannot do that until we first love ourselves. And we have value, whether our sphere of influence is five, five hundred, or five million.

PRACTICAL TRUTHS TO POWERFULLY LEAD KNOWING YOU ARE ENOUGH

Engage but Don't be Overtaken by the World

As I reflect on things I have experienced in this role as a superintendent—the financial crisis, difficult personnel decisions or student issues, closing school for health or safety reasons—I feel that sometimes it is easiest to lead when you're facing the most challenging of times. Because it is right in front of you. You know what the problem is and how to address it, and/or what steps to take to start the process of resolving it. It is much more challenging (for me) to lead when things are good. My district is *great* academically. We're one of the highest-performing districts in Texas; our sixty-five graduates earn about $2–3 million in college scholarships. We make all-state band/choir, play at the state level in sports, earn the coveted Grand Champion Award at major stock shows, were a 2017 National Blue Ribbon campus, and have National Merit Scholars. So how do you take *that* to the next level? What steps do you take?

It's easy to let myself get lost in what everyone *else* is doing and forget what we are doing and have done. There are some days I can't even get on Twitter or LinkedIn or any other source that highlights the incredible ways others are leading because as I read these stories and tweets, I'm constantly thinking, *That is awesome; she/he is awesome; we're not doing that; I'm not doing that.*

I hadn't realized how false my negative thinking could be until I was having a conversation with my husband about another district and some hardship they were facing. I said casually, "I can't even imagine being in that position. How do you even overcome that? How do you lead through that?" He looked at me dumbfounded and asked, "Have you so quickly forgotten? Do you not remember? Remember where your district was financially compared to where they are now? How far you have taken this district? You can do anything. You can lead anywhere." Well, OK then!

Focus on YOUR Strengths, Not on Others' Gifts You Think You Should Have

I can get lost in my weaknesses and lose sight of my strengths. Leadership roles in general, and especially the superintendency, are lonely—some of the loneliest out there. I have friends in the business, but nine times out of ten when I reach for my phone to call a fellow superintendent, it is to ask how they staffed a certain position or if they've ever dealt with a specific personnel issue. But rarely do I share what I am struggling with. And to compound matters, I've already concluded that everyone is better in their role than I am in mine because of the twenty-eight-second phenomenally positive clip they shared on social media.

But we know that when we discuss things we struggle with, they lose their grip over us. When I became really honest with my superintendent friends and just laid my struggles out there, I started to make movement in these areas. Because I received not only love and grace but encouragement that I am not alone. We have to be able to engage with this world, but not be overtaken by it.

Know Yourself to Lead Yourself

Jeremie Kubicek, author of *The 100X Leader: How to Become Someone Worth Following*, put it this way: "Leading yourself means becoming self-aware; it's learning to look for and see issues in your own life before pointing them out in others."[2] We must intentionally learn about ourselves—our strengths and our weaknesses—to help us better understand who we are as leaders. This also helps us understand the leaders that make up our teams.

There are so many tools out there to help grow our own self-awareness (CliftonStrengths, Myers-Briggs 16 Personalities, Enneagram, a Leadership Circle Profile, Wiley's DiSC, 5 Voices, and the Flippen Group Leadership Blueprint, just to name a few).[3] Consider embedding self-discovery into your leadership practices.

Conclusion

When I first began writing this chapter, the title that kept running over and over in my mind was "Never Enough." Because sometimes our 5 percent comes from our deep struggle with whether we will ever be enough. But I realized while writing it that the title demanded to be "You Are Enough." In every difficult situation I have faced, whether a health pandemic, student tragedy, or financial crisis, I have been reminded that not only is my leadership critical, it was meant for such a time as this.[4]

---

2 Jeremie Kubicek, "10 Tips for Becoming a Leader Worth Following," January 10, 2017, https://jamybechler.com/wp-content/uploads/2017/01/10-Tips-Becoming-a-Leader-Worth-Following-Jeremie-Kubicek.pdf.

3 CliftonStrengths: https://www.gallup.com/cliftonstrengths/en/253868/popular-cliftonstrengths-assessment-products.aspx; Myers Briggs 16 Personalities: https://www.16personalities.com/; Enneagram: https://www.enneagraminstitute.com/type-descriptions; Leadership Circle Profile: https://leadershipcircle.com/en/products/leadership-circle-profile/; 5 Voices: https://5voices.com/; Flippen Group Leadership Blueprint: https://flippengroup.com/education/leadership-blueprint/.

4 Esther 4:14

- YOU are where you are for a reason.
- YOU are sitting in the chair making decisions for your district.
- YOU are the one who is present in this time of challenge.
- YOU are the best person for this job—because of your strengths *and* because of what you are learning through your weaknesses.

Step out of your comfort zone, be faithful to what is before you, continue to take the next best step, give voice to your greatest hopes and dreams, let go of the world's perception, and keep doing great things! Because YOU are enough!

YOU ARE ENOUGH! STEP OUT OF YOUR COMFORT ZONE. GIVE VOICE TO YOUR GREATEST HOPES AND DREAMS. **LET GO OF THE WORLD'S PERCEPTION. GO DO GREAT THINGS!**

5 TIPS TO THRIVE

1 Take a reprieve from social media. Or check out the screen time features on your smart phone and at least become aware of how much time you're spending online. Better yet, set a schedule for your social media and stick to it!

2 Check in with a friend or colleague and go beyond the surface. Ask how they're really doing. Maybe even share a struggle and ask for their thoughts.

3 Ask yourself if there are any "never enough" areas in your life. Things where no matter how much or how well you do, it won't be enough. Try to put healthy parameters in place around those things.

4 Decide what needs to be "dead" to you. Unjoining a social media group that is constantly fraught with drama or half-truths? Coming face-to-face with some unhealthy habits in your life? Choosing your relationships more wisely or lovingly setting some boundaries in others? Love yourself enough to take care of you!

5 Keep a running record of your successes. When you begin to doubt, dig deep into those feelings to find if there are truly areas where you can grow. Take a lap around your victories to remember that you are unstoppable.

You alone are enough.
-Oprah Winfrey

You Are Enough
Thrive Through the Five by Jill M. Siler

Engage but Don't Be Overtaken by the World

PROCEED WITH CAUTION!

Social Media Envy · Your Story · Struggles

Know Yourself to Lead Yourself

learn yourself

Focus on Your Strengths, Not on Others' Gifts You Think You Should Have

share your struggles

TRUTH · TRUTH

All About ME

Better understand who we are as leaders

We have to find a way to engage with the world but not be overtaken by how that world receives us.

sketchnote by Amelia Buchanan
@edtech_amelia

FRAMEWORK TO THRIVE: YOU ARE ENOUGH

What are the frequent-flyer doubts that continue to bubble up in your life?	*As you reflect on your journey, what truths take the life out of those doubts?*
In what ways do you tend to get over-taken by the world?	*How can you set healthy parameters to offset those tendencies?*

How does the understanding that YOU are enough better help you think about thriving in the 5 percent?

PART III

LEADING OUT . . . .

What outward strategies can we use to lead through the 5 percent of our work and life that is really difficult?

What personal or professional change could we make that will help us better thrive?

How can we better think about decision-making, inspiring hope, engaging around contentious issues, leading from vision, taking our next best step, and using time in order to *thrive* through the most difficult 5 percent of what we do?

EIGHT

OUR ACTIONS MATTER

I have come to the frightening conclusion that I am the decisive element. It is my personal approach that creates the climate. It is my daily mood that makes the weather. I possess tremendous power to make life miserable or joyous. I can be a tool of torture or an instrument of inspiration, I can humiliate or humor, hurt or heal. In all situations, it is my response that decides whether a crisis is escalated or de-escalated, and a person is humanized or dehumanized. If we treat people as they are, we make them worse. If we treat people as they ought to be, we help them become what they are capable of becoming.

—HAIM G. GINOTT

That quote is frequently talked about in the realm of teaching, but each sentence is applicable to leadership as well. We are the decisive element in the cultures we create, the relationships we build, and the decisions we make. We can make our work environments miserable or joyous. We can humiliate, humor, hurt, or help heal the people we are entrusted to work with.

So many decision points come to mind when I reflect on my years as a superintendent. Just a few months into the job, I received a call informing me that earlier in the day, a group of children had been exiting the school bus when two pit bulls with a history of aggressive behavior came running toward them. The bus driver quickly called the children back on the bus, but only two were able to make it. The third ran to a house, and a parent came out to escort the other children inside. The dogs came at him. The parent pulled a gun and shot the dogs in self-defense—in front of the bus full of children. What is the school's role in this? How much should be communicated and to whom?

When the Ebola crisis was happening in the States, the first death in Texas happened at a Dallas hospital an hour away from our school district. That afternoon it was reported that family members of the deceased patient had gone to an area clinic for treatment and been transported to a Dallas hospital out of an abundance of caution. And one of our parents was leading the emergency medical response team as the patient was being prepared for transfer. Again, what is the school's role when information travels more quickly through a small town than through a metroplex media outlet? What decisions need to be made to ensure student safety and to calm community concern? The decisions we contemplated and the processes we put into place were critical preparation points for the dire challenges we would face with the 2017–18 flu outbreak and the 2020 COVID-19 pandemic.

Each year we have cycles of influenza across the country, but no year was like 2017–18 for Texas.[1] With over ten thousand deaths (an increase of 27 percent from the year prior and 82 percent from the year before that), it was widespread and dangerous. We had noticed an uptick of cases heading into our winter break and were so thankful for the time off to hopefully stall the spread. We had only been back a few days when the number of students diagnosed with flu started to rise. Over the weekend we continued to hear about confirmed cases,

---

1   Lena Sun, "Flu Broke Records for Death, Illnesses in 2017–18, ew CDC Numbers Show," *Washington Post*, September 27, 2018, https://www. washingtonpost.com/national/health-science/last-years-flu-broke-records-for -deaths-and-illnesses-new-cdc-numbers-show/2018/09/26/97cb43fc-c0ed -11e8-90c9-23f963eea204_story.html.

and by the time we came back on the second Monday in January, we knew we were in trouble. Not only was the number of cases rising, our staff was beginning to be significantly impacted as well. We had heard about area schools closing for short periods, taking a long weekend to sanitize and to allow for the separation of students, but we also knew that the flu cycle was a lot longer than a long weekend.

By the time we got to our board meeting the next night, the numbers were staggering—over 20 percent of students were out districtwide. And when we returned to school on Wednesday, we had 27 percent absent across the district, with our elementary campus at nearly 40 percent and our middle school campus at over 30 percent absent. And out of the 194 absent at those two campuses, 141 were confirmed flu cases or had flu symptoms and were being tested. What decision do you make? What will the impact be for students, their families? What is in the best interest of students? How will this impact future decisions?

We made the bold decision to close schools not just for an additional day for deep cleaning but for an entire week. We had built strong relationships with our local health care providers, and their data helped us understand how significant the outbreak was in our area. Their feedback was to close schools long enough to break the cycle—a week. This forced us to mobilize a communication strategy for our students, parents, community, and local media. The message went beyond school closure; it was a plea to not engage with others. Again, these events served as preparation for the coronavirus pandemic that was to come.

Tough decisions come at us every day. And our actions will have impact—for better and for worse. Every decision we make is "for" kids and our communities, but rarely is there a clear or easy answer as to what that *best* decision is. Our decisions often draw media attention as well. In all three of these cases, there were media requests and interviews. Most notably, when we closed the district for our flu crisis (known by those infected as "Flumaggedon" and, conversely, by those who never got the flu as "flucation"), I gave several local interviews.

That footage ended up on all of the local news outlets along with ABC's *World News Tonight* and the *Today Show*, and then led to a live segment on CNN's *Headline News*. I had to defend my decision and was ready to do so. Every decision we make has to be framed in the context of past knowledge, present circumstances, and all possible future implications and impact. So how do we do that? How do we know that our actions are the right ones and that they matter?

PRACTICAL TRUTHS TO POWERFULLY LEAD IN OUR ACTIONS

The Best Solution Is Better than Your Solution

It is important to seek common ground and lead toward the best solution. In difficult times it is easy to say "set the policy and uphold the policy," but life is not always black and white. Every situation is different—there are different contexts, different levels of information available, and different histories involved. The best solution is often found after seeking information, and engaging in dialogue and thoughtful deliberation. Be open to finding a place to meet in the middle, so long as it doesn't compromise what's best for kids or your integrity. One of my mentors, the late Dr. James Smith, a longtime superintendent, used to say, "If the decision was easy, it would have been made long before ending up on my desk."

Oftentimes, our job as leaders is to work in the gray. Another mentor and former superintendent, Dr. Jenny Preston, always shared a story about firefighters: as they approached a large fire, the chief and his or her team would look at the whole expanse of the fire before turning away to develop a plan. In other words, if we fixate solely on the problem before us, it's hard to find the remedy. Dr. Preston said, "If the decision before you is gray, withdraw from it and let your intuition mull it over before stepping back into the action of making the decision." When confronted with something messy, don't go for the quick solution; instead, seek every piece of information, try to understand the situation from every angle, and lead toward the best solution.

WHEN CONFRONTED WITH SOMETHING MESSY, DON'T GO FOR THE QUICK SOLUTION. TRY TO UNDERSTAND THE SITUATION FROM EVERY ANGLE AND LEAD TOWARD THE BEST SOLUTION.

Elizabeth Grace Saunders, international time management expert, recommends three steps to arrive at the best decision. First, schedule time to think. She notes, "It's counterintuitive, but making decisions faster requires consciously giving yourself time to make them."[2] Second, she recommends defining the decision before you make it, outlining all of the factors and contexts involved. And finally, think through all of the options, compromises, and alternatives possible before settling on the main solution.

Gain the Best Perspective

One of the best things you can do in challenging moments is to gain better perspective. There is no greater tool to de-escalate your own emotions when confronted with an upset parent, student, staff member, board member, community member—you name it—than to *truly* try to see and understand their perspective. When we can place the

---

2   Elizabeth Grace Saunders, "Five Ways to Make Tough Decisions Faster (and Not Regret Them Later)," *Fast Company*, July 12, 2018, https://www. fastcompany.com/90199653/5-ways-to-make-tough-decisions-faster-and-not -regret-them-later.

anger of someone who is confronting us in their context, we can often understand their frustration. They may not be addressing it in the most appropriate way, but that perspective can soften our normal defense mechanisms and allow for a path forward.

THERE IS NO GREATER TOOL TO DE-ESCALATE EMOTIONS WHEN CONFRONTED WITH SOMEONE WHO IS UPSET THAN TO TRULY **TRY TO SEE AND UNDERSTAND THEIR PERSPECTIVE.**

Part of that is also gaining a better perspective of the problem at hand. The aim is not simply to de-escalate; it's to truly understand if there really is a problem and then to partner with the person to find the best answers and solutions. As we have approached really challenging issues, from school safety to vaping to creating a welcoming and open environment for all students, we have tried to step back and really see and hear the perspectives of others so that *we* can become better.

It is important to recognize that not all feedback is created equal. In *Lead Like a Pirate: Make School Amazing for Your Students and Staff*, Shelley Burgess and Beth Houf frame criticism this way:

> There are two forms of criticism: constructive and destructive. Constructive criticism is offered by people who truly want to help you succeed. The insights that accompany constructive criticism can help make you and your school better and can help you to recalculate if you've gone off course . . . The goals of (destructive) critics are usually to

hurt both the people and the mission of the organization . . . These critics can be bullies and tend to cause drama, which completely takes away from the important work we do.[3]

Part of our work as leaders is to lean into the conflict to gain the best perspective we possibly can. Discern whether criticism is constructive or destructive in nature. Find ways that you or your organization can become better through conflicts.

Don't Avoid Problems

This next one is tough, especially for people who loathe confrontation as much as I do (and who loves confrontation, anyway?!), but we have to understand that as leaders, dealing with difficult (even ugly) situations is part of the job. Don't avoid problems. Kerry Patterson shared in *Crucial Confrontations*, "Sometimes we confront a problem at the wrong time or in the wrong way, but that's not the predominant issue in most families and companies. Going to silence is the prominent issue in these situations."[4] Jon Gordon adds, "One of the biggest mistakes leaders make is that they ignore the negativity within their team and organization. They allow it to breed and grow, and it eventually sabotages the team and organization."[5] Avoiding problems will only make them worse. That personnel situation (or financial situation or student discipline issue or fill in the blank) that you're magically hoping will just improve on its own?!? Probably not going to happen.

Joe Sanfelippo, speaker, author, and superintendent of Fall Creek, Wisconsin, shares #1minwalk2work leadership challenges. One of these challenges is about setting clear expectations for people. He

---

3   Shelley Burgess and Beth Houf, *Lead Like a Pirate: Make School Amazing for Your Students and Staff* (San Diego, Dave Burgess Consulting, Inc., 2017).

4   Kerry Patterson, Joseph Grenny, Ron McMillan, and Al Switzler, *Crucial Confrontations: Tools for Resolving Broken Promises, Violated Expectations, and Bad Behavior* (New York: McGraw-Hill, 2005).

5   Jon Gordon, *The Power of Positive Leadership* (New York: Wiley, 2017).

noted, "I hide behind the idea that 'people should just know' . . . without setting the clear expectation of what it looks like." Sometimes we avoid problems by shying away from actually vocalizing the expectation itself. Sanfelippo goes on to say:

> If we truly believe that people are doing the best that they know how, then we have to be willing to help with the how. And if I get frustrated with someone for not meeting an expectation that they don't know about, then the only person I can be frustrated with in that scenario is me.[6]

At the same time, don't delegate away something that is appropriate for you to lead through. That's why you get paid. Own it and lead through it.

DON'T DELEGATE AWAY SOMETHING THAT IS APPROPRIATE FOR YOU TO LEAD THROUGH. OWN IT AND LEAD THROUGH IT.

Remember to Lead

Often when challenging situations occur we move into reactionary mode, but that is when our leadership is needed the most. Leaders are sometimes called on to make difficult decisions in stressful situations, often with limited information. Hindsight may be 20/20, but it's not a viable lens for operating in the present. Use hindsight as a learning tool for the future but not as an unfair and destructive weapon against yourself! Learn from past mistakes. Use that learning

---

6   Joe Sanfelippo, "Leadership Challenge—Week 30," http://www.jsanfelippo.com/leadership-challenge.

to become a better leader and keep your focus on the wide expanse in front of you.

HINDSIGHT MAY BE 20/20, BUT WE OPERATE IN THE PRESENT. USE HINDSIGHT AS A LEARNING TOOL FOR THE FUTURE BUT NOT AS A WEAPON AGAINST YOURSELF.

Conclusion

I was talking with author Melanie Mayer about that difficult 5 percent, and she mentioned the story of Shadrach, Meshach, and Abednego. Those three young men refused to bow down to the king's image, aware that they would be thrown into a fiery furnace for doing so. They were indeed thrown into the furnace, yet survived unscathed.[7]

Melanie shared in our conversation that within the 5 percent exists a choice we have to make. She went on to say, "We want God to deliver us *from* the furnace, but He wants to deliver us *in* it." In this work we will face a choice of whether to walk into a fiery furnace. Whether that is for standing up for what is right for kids (regardless of the consequences) or simply because we're choosing to do the really hard work, sometimes we have to go to some dark places to do what we're called to do. But as Melanie reminded me, "That's where our legacy is made. That's what we talk about when we are eighty. [The most challenging work] is the work that defines our lives." [8]

---

7   Daniel 3:1-30

8   Melanie Mayer is an award-winning classroom teacher, college professor, author, and presenter. She has written *Miles to Go: What I Learned While I Was Teaching* and *Two Roads Diverged* and *I Took Both: Meaningful Writing Instruction in an Age of Testing*. Visit her website at www.melaniemayerconsulting.com.

5 TIPS TO THRIVE

1   Avoid making a quick decision just for the sake of making a decision. If it is messy, hit pause. Broaden your perspective on the situation. See if there are other facts that can be uncovered. Find the best solution or strategy even if it is not the easiest to implement or live with.

2   Listen to understand, not to defend. The next time you notice the tension rising, sit back, breathe, ask more questions, and truly try to understand the other person's perspective.

3   Every day, think about the thing that is causing you the most angst. Prepare for that and address it first. Get yourself in the habit of tackling the hard things first.

4   When someone is not meeting expectations, consider whether they understand them. If there's a chance they don't, start there. Clarify your expectations and offer tangible support to help achieve them.

5   Recognize the next time you are standing before a fiery furnace. If it is the right thing to do for kids, make the choice to step in.

> I have come to the frightening conclusion that I am the decisive element. It is my personal approach that creates the climate. It is my daily mood that makes the weather. —Haim G Ginott

SO MANY DECISIONS

- ★ Hard personal conversations
- ★ Student Mental Health
- ★ Global Pandemic
- ★ School closure decisions
- ★ Contentious parent meetings
- ★ Student safety

Our Actions Matter

Thrive Through the Five by Jill M. Siler

☑ The Best Solution Is Better than Your Solution

LEAD toward the BEST SOLUTION!

COMMON GROUND

☑ Gain the Best Perspective

Step back and really see and hear the perspective of others so that WE can become BETTER

☑ Don't Avoid Problems

OWN IT and LEAD THROUGH IT

UGLY SITUATIONS

AVOIDING PROBLEMS ONLY MAKES IT WORSE

☑ Remember to Lead

HINDSIGHT is 20/20 LEARNING TOOL FOR THE FUTURE

Lead Your Best Way

As leaders, we are the decisive element in the cultures we create, the relationships we build, and the decisions we make.

Sketchnote by Amelia Buchanan
@edtech_amelia

FRAMEWORK TO THRIVE: ACTIONS

Think back to the last difficult decision you had to make . . .		
What was your gut reaction about what you should do to solve it?	*What action did you ultimately take?*	*What did you learn through that decision and its impact?*

How do you gain a better perspective when facing a difficult decision?	*What strategies do you use to ensure that you don't avoid problems?*

How does the understanding that our actions matter in decision-making help you think about thriving in the 5 percent?

INSPIRE HOPE

*Hope begins in the dark, the stubborn hope
that if you just show up and try to do the
right thing, the dawn will come. You wait and
watch and work: you don't give up.*

—ANNE LAMOTT

Finding that perfect fit for your family can be challenging. When looking to transition into the superintendency, I researched *everything* about the districts I was considering. The tipping point for Gunter ISD came through reading their *Tiger Times*,[1] a monthly newsletter that highlights classroom events, student success stories, and community activities. It was one of a dozen things I reviewed (board agendas/minutes, accountability reports, financial audits, bond overviews, etc.) before making a decision on whether to apply. I remember saying to my husband, "This could be the one—I could see our family here," as we read the March edition of the newsletter and looked at pictures from the Daddy-Daughter Dance and other events they had hosted the month before.

But just a few nights later, I came back and said, "We need to talk." As my research became more detailed, I had begun to see some signs

---

1   The Gunter ISD monthly newsletter, *The Tiger Times*, can be found at: https://www.gunterisd.org/newsletter.

of financial distress within the district. I had gathered all of my data and shared it with a fellow CFO, and he had called that night to confirm my fears. I always encourage others when they are considering new job opportunities to view the interviewing process as seriously as one would contemplate marriage. You can't just focus on getting the job; you need to focus on having the job and whether it is a fit for your strengths and skill set. This was one of those moments. After I walked into the living room and told my husband the dire financial situation I was seeing, he asked just one question: "Can you fix it?" I said yes, but that it was going to be really difficult. He replied, "Then I'm all in."

I loved meeting the board members in the first interview, and toward the end of my second interview, one of the board members asked, "Jill, if the state continues to cut funding and financial conditions continue to deteriorate, will you be able to make the difficult decisions necessary?" I answered that it was not a matter of *if* but a matter of *when* and asked if I could walk them through why I thought so and how I would lead the district through it. Thirty minutes later, I was named lone finalist for the district.

That year, I learned some important lessons about leading through crisis. All of us face significant challenges in the work we do; mine just happened to be financial. But I will carry the lessons I learned that year with me forever. The greatest among these was how to inspire hope through challenging times.

PRACTICAL TRUTHS TO POWERFULLY LEAD THROUGH HOPE

Anchor Your Decisions and Story in Facts and Data

The first key to leading through a crisis is to anchor your decisions and story in facts and data. We had a perfect storm of financial challenges: declining enrollment, decreasing property values, historic reductions in state funding, a tax rate that was maxed out, and a fund balance that was too low to help mitigate any future losses. To add insult to injury, the neighboring K–8 district, for which we had been the receiving district for high school students, opened up their own high school. While their school community celebrated, ours experienced complete financial devastation. In Texas schools, funding comes from several places, including local funds and property taxes, but the main factor is student enrollment. The more students you have, the more funding you receive. So to lose an entire group of students was a devastating loss (about $1.5 million in just the first four years).

When a crisis occurs, it is crucial to have a complete understanding of what is happening and why, not only so you can make it better but so that you can communicate it to others. Share the gravity of the situation, but do not exaggerate the facts. It is important to try to withhold judgment and simply make the situation better. Hindsight is a gift not available to the person making decisions in the present—they know only the data they have before them. In my situation, the prior leadership had made massive strides to overcome the deteriorating financial conditions. When facing crisis, be really clear about the facts of the situation and then anchor decisions and communication in those facts.

Paint a Picture

The second key to leading through challenging times is to paint a picture of the context of the situation. My dad began his career as a janitor, moved his way up to factory assembly-line worker, and finished his career as the CEO of several companies—all without ever going to college. His extraordinary success was due in part to the fact that he was masterful at painting a picture: taking extremely complex information and simplifying it in such a way that anyone could understand or remember it, or share it with a neighbor or friend.

That was my task—to take the overwhelmingly complex world of school finance and explain the facts in such a way that they were easily understandable. I did this through simple but significant graphics, simple but informative words, and a simple but substantive message.

My goal in my meetings with the board, our leadership team, our staff, and our community was for them to be able to walk away and tell a neighbor exactly why we were in the situation we were in. It was critical that they understood what had happened, why it had happened, and what would happen if we didn't take steps to rectify the situation.

Lay a Path

The next key difference between managing a crisis and leading through a crisis is your ability to lay a path. It is irresponsible for leaders to share devastating news without also including a path for how to move forward, for how to be successful through it. The path doesn't have to be worked out completely—in fact, the path can simply be the steps you're going to take to attempt to solve the problem itself. But whenever possible, anytime bad news is given, it should be accompanied by the next steps you'll take to try to overcome the issue, and the information should be grounded in the belief that it can be done and done well.

> IT IS IRRESPONSIBLE FOR LEADERS TO SHARE DEVASTATING NEWS WITHOUT ALSO INCLUDING A PATH FOR HOW TO MOVE FORWARD, FOR HOW TO BE SUCCESSFUL THROUGH IT.

Our path included generating as much revenue as possible, increasing attendance and enrollment, and cutting nonpersonnel costs as much as possible. Our goal was to build back the financial integrity of the district while at the same time protecting the instructional integrity of the classroom.

Jon Gordon shares that "leadership is a transfer of belief. What you believe is possible, and the beliefs you share with your team and organization have a big influence on what you create, build, accomplish."[2] Hope happens when we transfer our belief that we can thrive through this challenging time to others.

HOPE HAPPENS WHEN WE TRANSFER OUR BELIEF THAT WE CAN THRIVE THROUGH CHALLENGING TIMES TO OTHERS.

One delicate part of communication is determining exactly what to share. Kevin Hub, a superintendent from Kentucky, notes:

> A crucial element of transparency is figuring out just how open to be—just how much to hang on the line for all to see—for while there can be too little transparency, there also can be too much. When transparency is employed without a keen understanding of the potential effects of revealed information, it can be unfair and irresponsible both to the organization and to its individual members.[3]

It would have been easier and faster for me to say everything at once, to all parties at once. But it was more effective to make sure my board understood every facet of our challenges and to then share layers of information in conjunction with steps for how we were going to work through each piece as we went. From a logistical standpoint, it looked like this: whole group board meetings followed by individual meetings with board members; leadership team meetings followed

---

2   Jon Gordon, *The Power of Positive Leadership* (New York: Wiley, 2017).

3   Kevin Hub, "Leadership & Transparency: Part II," January 10, 2014, https://kevinhub.wordpress.com/2014/01/10/leadership-transparency-part-ii/.

by small-group strategy sessions; full faculty meetings followed by individual meetings at campuses; large community forums followed by smaller meetings at the coffee shop.

The truth was that, given that 85 percent of the budget is in personnel, in facing a financial crisis as significant as ours there was no way to avoid impacting personnel. We tried to do so with as much dignity and grace as possible, offering financial incentives for notice of early resignation to give our staff as much ownership as possible. The day we started accepting those early notices of resignation was one of the most emotional days I've had as superintendent. Incredible teachers and staff members gave up their own jobs so that their colleagues, friends, their family, did not have to lose theirs. Their sacrificial gift accounted for 80 percent of what was needed to reduce our budget, and it happened in large part because of their love for their work family (fostered by great leaders before me) and because the financial challenges had been so clearly laid out before them.

Lead with Heart

I shared earlier the difference between managing and leading through a crisis. I believe that the difference between leading through a crisis and inspiring hope through those moments is to lead with heart. As an aspiring superintendent, I dreamed about my first convocation. One of the greatest privileges of serving as superintendent is being able to set the tone for the organization. But in addition to sharing my excitement about the possibilities within this new district, I also was tasked with delivering sobering news about the financial challenges we were facing. I did so using the steps above: painting a clear picture of where we were and how we got there, laying out a path of how we could and would overcome the crisis, and sharing how I would communicate every step of the way. Even though I was new to them, I cared so deeply for the district, and I was all in with them. I had a teacher come up to me after that very first session and share that she hoped she never got cancer, but that if she did, she hoped that I was the person who told her the news. Because she had never heard more devastating news and been more encouraged at the same time.

As James Kouzes and Barry Posner share in *The Truth about Leadership*, "The best leaders are like that. They define the reality of illness, but defy the verdict that we are doomed."[4] That is our job as leaders, to inspire hope through challenging times. Our calling is to let people know that we will be able to not just survive but also thrive through those moments.

OUR JOB AS LEADERS IS TO INSPIRE HOPE THROUGH CHALLENGING TIMES, TO LET PEOPLE KNOW THAT WE WILL NOT JUST SURVIVE BUT CAN AND WILL THRIVE!

I hated the decisions that we were facing, but I had also fallen in love with that community. Anyone could have come in and fixed the problem; it wasn't a question of *what* to do. I don't know, though, that just anyone could have come in and led through it in the way that I did, because it was done with heart. I've shared often that the twelve most important inches in leadership are those between the head and the heart. It's not just about what to do, it's *how* we do it and *why* we do it. As the leader, you have the privilege to make the best decisions you can to help your organization thrive through crisis.

The journey was difficult, and it wasn't perfect. There are moments I replay over and over again, wishing I had done something differently. But the year we made those decisions, and in the years

---

4   James M. Kouzes and Barry Z. Posner, *The Truth About Leadership: The No-Fads, Heart-of-the-Matter Facts You Need to Know* (San Francisco, Jossey-Bass, 2010).

after, where we had to learn to live with the impact of those decisions (decreased staffing, reduced funding, increased student counts, etc.), our staff rose up, and our staff and students truly thrived! Our district is now squarely on the road to financial health; we have added back a dozen positions and rebuilt our fund balance, and we are very thankful to have been able to give compensation increases for several years running.

Conclusion

I shared this quote by Anne Lamott at the beginning of the chapter: "Hope begins in the dark, the stubborn hope that if you just show up and try to do the right thing, the dawn will come. You wait and watch and work: you don't give up."[5] Hope might not be a strategy for improvement, but hope is absolutely necessary in the midst of a crisis. It fosters the belief that the organization can endure the challenge and reminds people why they do what they do and how valuable they are in doing that.

Facing a crisis is not a matter of if, it's a matter of when. But if you approach the situation anchored by the facts of the reality you're facing, if you're able to paint a picture of where you are and where you need to be, while laying out a path of how you can get there, and if you lead through it all with love, you can truly inspire hope through those challenging times!

> HOPE MIGHT NOT BE A STRATEGY FOR IMPROVEMENT, **BUT HOPE IS ABSOLUTELY NECESSARY IN LEADING THROUGH CRISIS.**

---

5   Anne Lamott, *Bird by Bird: Some Instructions on Writing and Life* (New York: Penguin Random House, 1994).

5 TIPS TO THRIVE

1   When sharing difficult news about a complex issue, focus on simplicity in your message. When you feel like you have a solid approach to communicate, start with someone without intimate knowledge around the issue to measure your clarity.

2   Think about taking a tiered approach to communication, beyond why something happened. Reflect on what happened, why it happened, and what will happen if the situation is not rectified—along with your thoughts on how to solve it.

3   Consider what information is appropriate to share and what is not. Irresponsible transparency is not the goal. Be discerning about what is appropriate to share in order to provide clarity in difficult times.

4   To transfer belief to others, you must first believe. Before moving forward with a strategy, make sure you are all in with that approach.

5   Above all, remind people why they do what they do and how valuable they are in achieving the purpose of your organization.

Hope begins in the dark, the stubborn hope that if you just show up to do the right thing the dawn will come. You wait and watch and work, you don't give up. – Anne Lamott

Inspire Hope

Thrive Through the Five by Jill M. Siler

Anchor Your Decisions & Story in Facts and Data

STORY
DECISIONS

Paint a Picture

CONTEXT

What — HOW — When
Why

The 12 most important inches in leadership are those between the **head** and the **heart.**

Lay a Path

TRANSFER
BELIEF TRANSFER
TRANSFER BELIEF
BELIEF TRANSFER

Lead with Heart

Our job as leaders is to inspire hope through challenging times; to let people know that we will not just survive but <u>can</u> and <u>will</u> *thrive.*

Sketchnote by Amelia Buchanan
@edtech_amelia

FRAMEWORK TO THRIVE: INSPIRING HOPE

When you come upon a crisis or a challenging time, what are your initial reactions and emotions?	*How do you ground yourself to face the situation?*

Think about one challenging time that you have gone through . . .

How did you or whoever was leading ground the crisis in facts, paint a clear picture, and lay out a path?	*How were you or they able to convey hope in the midst of the challenging time?*

How does understanding the importance of inspiring hope in challenging times help you think about thriving in the 5 percent?

TEN

ENGAGE AROUND CONTENTIOUS ISSUES

*There is a difference between listening
and waiting for your turn to speak.*

—SIMON SINEK

As a school district, we have always focused on student safety and looking at every way we can make our schools safer for students. But in 2018, after the Parkland tragedy, emotions were exceedingly high. Districts were already years into massive improvements in safety infrastructure but began to look once more at every facet of school safety with fresh eyes. We live in a rural area, where there are miles and miles between police departments, and schools in our area began to train and arm their teachers as an additional layer of defense.

People drew hard lines on whether that was an appropriate role for school staff. Many felt that every campus had a small number of people who had unique backgrounds (military/law enforcement) who would be capable of this or that the district could find substantial training for them to be able to be effective in this capacity. Others wondered if any level of training would be enough in a situation like that and worried about the possible ramifications if a teacher or staff member were ever to inadvertently injure a child in the process.

At the same time, an #armmewith movement began across the country,[1] where teachers shared on social media what they truly wanted to be armed with, saying things like: "#ArmMeWith books . . . because our six-year-olds need to learn to read, not be scared in class," or "#ArmMeWith the resources and funding needed to help students experiencing mental health issues,"[2] or "#ArmMeWith full-time social workers and counselors. Arm me with more contact time with students that doesn't revolve around test scores. Arm me with support from both sides of the aisle because thoughts and prayers should lead to change and reform." And just to lighten the mood for a second, my personal favorite, "#ArmMeWith school supplies. Literally. I should not be single-handedly keeping Target in business."[3]

Our own community and school board were split in their feelings, and there was great angst about whether we were doing "enough" to protect our students. Our leadership team knew that the best way to resolve concerns and find our best way forward was to bring in the community. But how do you do that around an issue so contentious that even your own staff, leadership team, and school board are not in agreement?

There are always two choices in leadership. You can become defensive and state erroneously that you are "doing everything you can." Or you can engage. Even if it means recognizing that there is more you can be doing. Even if it means realizing that there is more that you should be doing. Even if it means becoming vulnerable. If we are going to truly thrive through the really difficult moments, we must learn to engage with others, especially in the midst of a contentious issue.

---

1   Amanda Morris, "In #ArmMeWith Movement, Teachers Ask to Be Armed—But Not with Guns," CNN, February 22, 2018, https://www.cnn.com/2018/02/22/politics/armmewith-twitter-teachers-guns/index.html.

2   Brittany Jeltema, Instagram, February 20, 2018, https://www.instagram.com/p/BfcBVaAHlB2/?taken-by=thesuperheroteacher.

3   Olivia Bertels, Instagram, February 20, 2018, https://www.instagram.com/p/BfcO3jQhBtU/?taken-by=missbertels.

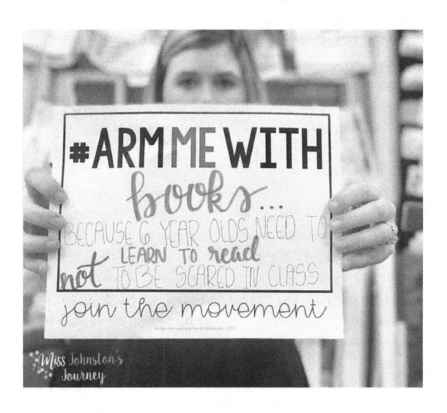

THERE IS ALWAYS A CHOICE IN LEADERSHIP. YOU CAN BECOME DEFENSIVE, OR YOU CAN LEAN IN AND ENGAGE. EVEN IF THAT MEANS BECOMING VULNERABLE.

My board and I knew we wanted to engage the community around this issue. That's great in theory but really *hard* in practice. One of our area districts had just hosted a safety and security community forum, recorded the entire event, and shared it online. I opened my laptop, clicked on the link, and sat back to watch as this awesome district shared the incredible actions they were taking. And yet as the meeting was coming to a close, people were upset and angry and frustrated—to the point where one person came up on stage and took over the meeting.

I leaned forward, closed the laptop, and said out loud, "I'm out." There was no way I was going to go through with this forum idea. Here was a district that did so many things right: they addressed the issue from all angles (from infrastructure to emotional wellness), they included multiple experts to share information (from district operations personnel to counselors to area law enforcement), and they allowed time for audience participation (through an open Q&A at the end). And yet, for all intents and purposes, the meeting went off the rails.

I sat quietly for a few moments, honestly wondering how I could get out of doing this, and then opened the laptop again, took out a notebook, hit Play one more time, and began to take notes. I realized that I had been given an incredible gift in watching and learning from this so that I could help our community and share it with others. I began to think about how to design a time for purposeful engagement; how to share our story in a way that allowed us to discuss the great steps we had taken but also acknowledge the areas that needed improvement. How we could engage in meaningful dialogue where we didn't just talk but also listened intently. And then how to follow up in a way that our community knew we used their voice to improve what we were doing.

PRACTICAL TRUTHS TO POWERFULLY ENGAGE THROUGH CONTENTIOUS ISSUES

Design Purposeful Experiences

We spent time purposefully designing a community forum that provided meaningful experiences and discussions among our community members. That meant thoughtful design, setting clear expectations, and providing varied activities.

Our community deserved the same kind of **thoughtful design** that we would put into planning a learning experience for kids or our staff. The design started with how we set up the room. We set up our meeting space, using round tables instead of traditional rows to foster dialogue. We set *Reserved* signs on all of the tables along the perimeter to force people to fill up interior tables and removed signs as we needed additional tables. This process resulted in diverse groupings across the room. We included a trained discussion facilitator at every table. These facilitators included campus and district leaders, school board members, counselors, and community leaders. In the same respect, we also made sure we had all the voices in the room that we needed.

One of the most purposeful things we did that night was to **set clear expectations** around the kind of dialogue we desired. We acknowledged that what we were about to talk about was the most precious thing we could—the safety and well-being of our children—and asked attendees to commit to allowing everyone at the table an opportunity to talk; to listen to one another's ideas and seek to understand other people's point of view; and most importantly, to be respectful when disagreeing, because there was going to be disagreement in the midst of everything we were discussing. One of our families in town had recently been trained in Safe Conversations® by Relationships First, an organization whose mission is to empower people to talk and listen with mutual respect and real connection. They shared with us their motto that "talking is the most dangerous thing people do." So, we spent time talking about how we were going to talk. We then made sure to **vary our content** (from safety infrastructure to social and emotional health) and to **vary our activities** (from informational presentations to thought-provoking videos on gun violence warning signs[4] to discussion time to an expert panel).

IT'S NOT ENOUGH TO HAVE ALL THE VOICES IN A ROOM. WE NEED TO ENSURE THAT EVERY VOICE IS HEARD.

Tell Your Story

We wanted to make sure that our story was **well-rounded and grounded in facts and data**. Before the forum occurred, our leadership team designed a survey that asked our parents about their feelings around the safety of their children within our schools along with their greatest safety concerns. We then shared those data along with our district information, including the security upgrades we had made and plans that were in progress. We included information on our safety infrastructure improvements and talked about the work we were doing to address our students' social and emotional health. As we shared crucial changes we'd made to our infrastructure,[5] we also were **transparent** about the things that still needed improvement. We brought in a **panel of experts** that included our local police department, county sheriff, and state trooper to share their experience and training, then allowed the community to ask questions

---

4   Sandy Hook Promise: sandyhookpromise.org, on knowing the signs of gun violence. Also "Gun Violence Warning Signs": https://www.youtube.com/watch?v=9qyD7vjVfLI.

5   Infrastructure upgrades included security cameras on our campuses and buses, rebuilding an entrance to create a secure vestibule for our middle school campus, and redoing our entire phone system to ensure that every classroom had a stable communication system.

about how they would handle various situations. And we kept our **focus on the kids**, incorporating some of the incredible things they had been accomplishing and also including their voices at the table and in our surveys.

But it's more than just sharing the facts and data; it is the power in your story. Early in my leadership journey, I was blessed with incredible mentors, and the leader of my principal certification, David Manning, was one of them. As a brand-new assistant principal, I was desperately seeking pertinent information on effective master scheduling, developing disciplinary consequences charts, and designing meaningful and effective professional development for teachers. And he was talking about building deep and meaningful relationships with everyone you come into contact with. Over time he helped me see the big picture of leadership, including the power of storytelling. Now we have best-selling books like Kindra Hall's *Stories That Stick*,[6] but David was ahead of his time, teaching us about the power of connecting with others in a way that carries them on a journey through our words. That night we were able to tell the powerful story about how our entire community was coming together to help keep kids safe.

Engage in Meaningful Dialogue

The most important work we did that night was to engage our community in meaningful dialogue. We did that by structuring our conversation around purposeful work and **framing the discussion**. In our pre-survey, we asked about their top concerns around school safety in our district and then shared the top 10 with the large group. We included a list of possible solutions for every concern. These ranged from really easy to implement to nearly impossible and/or unwanted solutions and asked the table which solutions would be best for kids and if there were any solutions we were not thinking of. One example of a concern was our students traveling to and from campuses

6   Kindra Hall, *Stories That Stick: How Storytelling Can Captivate Customers, Influence Audiences, and Transform Your Business* (New York: HarperCollins Publishing, 2019).

throughout the day at our secondary schools. We have middle school students who walk on a sidewalk across a parking lot to our high school for classes (PE, band, choir, athletics) every period of the day. And high school students who walk to the fieldhouse, ag barn, horticulture garden, track and field, etc. So often, people will say to do "whatever it takes" when it comes to safety, but if you're really going to make a playground "safe," it would end up looking more like a prison than a place of play. We listed an entire range of options, from outdoor teacher supervision to hiring an armed officer to erecting a privacy fence to perimeter fencing to completely enclosing all outdoor walkways and then facilitated meaningful conversation around what were the best solutions for us.

We created **opportunities for dialogue**. The discussion facilitators asked what their table participants thought, asked questions, took notes, and fostered conversation to ensure that all voices were heard. Not only did our discussion facilitators take notes, but each participant was given a feedback form to collect individual feedback on the spot about what they heard that night—what they loved and what concerns remained. We then offered a space to volunteer for the safety and security task force that would take this work even further in the coming months. These **mechanisms for feedback** were critical in the process, as was **acknowledging difficult topics**. We shared that as deeply passionate as you felt about one thing, the person next to you might feel as deeply passionate about the exact opposite. We shared pictures of school signs of all of our area schools that were arming teachers and shared pictures of teachers across our country holding #armmewith signs that had nothing to do with guns.

Dr. Harville Hendrix, creator of Safe Conversations®, noted that people are going to disagree:

> So you're always going to disagree to some degree, from a very little to a lot. The best thing to do is to go back to that principle of curiosity. Instead of negating it, judging it, or making it bad, get curious. Curiosity opens you

up to see another point of view that you might not have seen before. You don't have to agree with their point of view, but if you allow them to have their point of view and include it in your worldview then your world enlarges and you become less rigid and more flexible because there is some diversity of thinking in your own mind.[7]

By acknowledging difficult topics and then talking about them, we not only diffused contentious conversations but allowed for meaningful dialogue and hopefully a wider perspective of others and the world.

ACKNOWLEDGE AND DISCUSS DIFFICULT TOPICS. IT WILL DIFFUSE CONTENTIOUS CONVERSATIONS, FOSTER MEANINGFUL DIALOGUE, AND WIDEN PERSPECTIVES.

Follow Up

One of the most frustrating parts of engaging in something is wondering whatever happened with it, so sharing next steps is critical. We shared our **next steps**, which included continuing our safety improvements, reviewing all of the feedback, and meeting with various groups (leadership team, school board, district advisory team, local law enforcement) to determine how to best move forward, convening a community safety and security task force and developing next steps to continue the work. We shared our timelines for when that work

---

7   Jenn Brown, "The Art of Listening: An Interview with Harville Hendrix and Helen LaKelly Hunt," Be Here Now Network, May 29, 2019, https://beherenownetwork.com/the-art-of-listening-an-interview-with-harville-hendrix-and-helen-lakelly-hunt/.

would occur. We also worked to **gather feedback** through our individual discussion cards and followed up with anyone who had specific questions or concerns. Finally, we made sure to **continue communicating** through our newsletter, an email to all participants, and emails to our staff and school community, and by including safety and security as a standing board agenda item.

Paul Axtell commented in the *Harvard Business Review* that two things you should always do after a meeting are "quickly send out clear and concise meeting notes and follow up on commitments made."[8] After our forum, that is exactly what we did by providing a full summary to our staff and school community on a variety of platforms, and then we followed up through the creation of a districtwide safety and security plan brought to life by our safety and security task force. Follow-up is key!

Conclusion

The truth is that there is no magic wand when it comes to difficult issues. Hard issues and contentious subjects are part of leadership. But when you acknowledge difficult topics and engage people around contentious issues through meaningful dialogue, amazing work can happen! You as a leader and your entire organization will be better off because of it.

As I write this chapter, we've just finished our Homecoming Week. This is a special time for any school community and especially for a small, one-high-school town like ours. It was everything you could want it to be: dress-up days for kids (and adults); a community tailgate where everyone comes out to find fellowship and enjoy free food that various businesses, churches, and organizations provide; a community pep rally under the lights complete with performances from our cheerleaders, from the younger kids to our varsity squad; music from our band and choir; and the revealing of our Homecoming Court. The

---

8   Paul Axtell, "Two Things to Do After Every Meeting," *Harvard Business Review*, November 26, 2015, https://hbr.org/2015/11/two-things-to-do-after-every -meeting.

night concluded with a fireworks show, with all of our high school students sitting on the blue-and-green football field with their friends while Kenny Chesney's epic "The Boys of Fall" played over the loudspeaker. Friday's festivities included a parade that literally shut down the highway that leads from Dallas to Oklahoma, a community barbecue dinner, and, of course, Tiger victories in volleyball and football.

Included in those festivities was the crowning of Homecoming King and Queen. This is always special, and our lineup this year was stellar, with seniors whose interests ranged as widely as the interests of our entire student body—from football to choir to cheerleading to robotics to the rodeo. All of them are incredible representatives of what it means to be a Gunter Tiger, and any would have been a fantastic choice for King or Queen.

One of these students was Angelica. Our high school principal wrote about her that "she has the voice of an angel and a heart of gold." She is not only a member of chamber choir but always brings the house down when she sings. Angelica was diagnosed with autism in middle school, and she has truly blossomed in our district. She is a friend to all and has become an advocate for autism awareness, even training some local preschool teachers to help them better understand how to support and help students like her thrive in their classrooms.

When Angelica was crowned Homecoming Queen, it was one of many moments during Homecoming Week that made me tear up. Her mom wrote a post about it after the week was over, and reading that brought a few more tears. Our community is special because of the people that make it up, and Angelica's mom wrote about all of the people that made that moment, and Angelica's life, special—from kindergarten to senior year.[9]

Living in community is beautiful. But living in community is also hard. None of us are perfect, and sometimes that means we get hurt. We get hurt by the negative social media post that goes viral even though it isn't necessarily steeped in truth. We struggle when we see

---

9   A huge thanks to Angelica's family for allowing me to share her incredible story.

people we care for hold opposite viewpoints and beliefs and don't see a way to bridge the gap. We get hurt by people we love and respect who make judgments around the work we're doing our very best to do well. But we as leaders have to realize that we don't get to enjoy the beautiful parts about living in community without doing the hard work to engage with others when issues arise. This work is never easy, but it is always right. The truth is, the same things that drew me to this district eight years ago are the same things that keep me here now. There will be challenges in every leadership role you hold; the joy comes when you love the people you are leading with and for.

5 TIPS TO THRIVE

1 The next time you find yourself in a contentious conversation, shut down your automatic defenses and try these powerful words: "Tell me more."

2 When planning for a community event, be intentional about ways to foster dialogue. That includes how you seat people, how you collect feedback, and how you structure the content and activities.

3 When sharing information around a contentious issue, remember to be transparent. Share the great things you are doing in that area and the tangible steps you've already taken. But also share the shortcomings and areas you're targeting for the future.

4 Know that we won't always handle contention well. Reflect on tough conversations. Admit when things didn't go well. Make amends.

5 Be sure to follow up after major meetings and events. It's not enough that you know everything you're doing. You have to communicate those steps with your community at large.

There is a difference between listening and waiting for your turn to speak.
-Simon Sinek

Engage Around Contentious Issues

Thrive Through the Five by Jill M. Siler

 Design Purposeful Experiences

 Tell Your Story

thoughtful design

VOICE

clear expectations

Varied activities

WELL-ROUNDED FACTS DATA

 Engage in Meaningful Dialogue

Follow Up

THE DISCUSSION

Foster a conversation

Acknowledge difficult topics

FRAME

SHARE NEXT STEPS

UPDATES
continue communicating

Gather Feedback

There is always a choice in leadership. You can become defensive, or you can lean in and engage, even if that means becoming vulnerable.

Sketchnote by Amelia Buchanan @edtech-amelia

FRAMEWORK TO THRIVE: ENGAGE

What is a contentious issue facing your community?	What concerns do you have about engaging others in this discussion?

Consider a topic in which you would like to engage the community. Brainstorm how you could facilitate meaningful dialogue within the four phases noted below.

Design Meaningful Experiences (use a thoughtful design, set clear expectations, vary activities)	Engage in Meaningful Discussion and Feedback (frame the discussion, provide opportunities for dialogue, create mechanisms for feedback, acknowledge difficult topics)

Tell Your Story (draw on well-rounded/ grounded info, encourage transparency, bring in experts, focus on kids)	Follow Up (discuss next steps, gather feedback, continue communicating)

How does having a framework to engage others help you think about thriving in the 5 percent?

ELEVEN

LEAD FROM VISION

Vision without action is merely a dream.
Action without vision just passes the time.
Vision with action can change the world.

—JOEL A. BARKER

I have the distinct honor of leading our convocation, or opening cer-
emony, with our district staff each year. Every year at this special
event, we reflect on successes from the previous year and celebrate
the incredible people who help make our district amazing every day,
and then I spend a few moments talking about our vision for the
upcoming year.

One of the greatest joys of being a leader is seeing others bring
the shared vision of an organization to life. I love visiting campuses
and seeing individual examples of what we are talking about come
to life through others' creative and unique ways of leading. Last year,
we had intentional focus on our strategic initiatives around innovative
learning, preparing future-ready students, and ensuring social and
emotional wellness. Our middle school principal shared a bingo board
complete with prizes, made up of tangible instructional strategies
around our innovative learning goal. My elementary principal took
this year's #2020vision and, using Jon Gordon's One Word, had teachers metal-stamp their one-word intentional commitment on bracelets

for the whole staff to wear.[1] My high school principal took our strategic plan's learner profile and empowered his teachers to brainstorm what that would look like in their classrooms and, more importantly, how we could make it better. Each of these examples underscores one thing: the vision of the leader matters.

Vision is, ironically, the one thing that almost kept me from the superintendency—both personally and professionally. There was a point in my journey where I thought I was open to my next best step, but I really wasn't. Then the author Jen Hatmaker came to speak at our church in the early days of her ministry.[2] She shared about being open to God's calling and her realization that sometimes her "yes" wasn't even on the table. I, too, *felt* like I was open to anything, but when I really started to reflect on it, I realized I was actually open to only a certain kind of job, with a certain kind of title, in a certain kind of district, with a certain kind of salary, in a certain kind of geographic location. Do you get the picture? It was as if I had taken the massive expanse of what could be (because each of us has a massive expanse of what could be in our lives) and drawn a small box around what I deemed possible. And the superintendency wasn't in it; it wasn't even on the table. My personal vision was small.

THE EXPANSE OF WHAT COULD BE IS MASSIVE. DON'T DRAW A SMALL BOX AROUND POSSIBILITY.

1   Dan Britton, Jimmy Page, and Jon Gordon, *One Word That Will Change Your Life* (New York: Wiley, 2013).

2   Jen Hatmaker is a funny, deep-thinking, bold, truth-telling speaker, teacher, and writer. Her most recent book, *Fierce, Free, and Full of Fire*, debuted at #2 on the New York Times best-seller list. Visit her website: jenhatmaker.com.

It wasn't just my limiting personal vision that was holding me back, it was lack of confidence in my professional vision. I was happily serving in a central office position when my superintendent suddenly stepped down. I hadn't really seen myself becoming superintendent until that point. Even on the first day of my superintendency-based doctoral program, as we sat in a large circle and had to introduce ourselves and say why we wanted to become superintendents, I remember thinking, *I'm going to have to lie.* I chose the program because it was an incredible school, and the program was truly grounded in theory and practice, but I had little intention of actually *becoming* a superintendent. But in that year when our superintendent departed, I had multiple people ask me if I was considering applying, and somehow things began to shift in my thinking. It wasn't that I could even be a candidate—that job was not a feasible starting point for me. But it was the first time that I really started to *think* about the possibility of becoming a superintendent, mostly due to the encouragement of others.

I still struggled, though, with envisioning myself in that role. I remember confiding some of these thoughts and fears with my assistant superintendent, and she was so affirming of me. But I persisted in my negativity, saying, "Yeah, but superintendents need to have qualities like vision." She responded with words that changed my life. She said, "Jill, you are one of the most visionary leaders I have ever known."

My response was silence. Not because I was flattered; not even because I was humbled. I was dumbfounded. You see, I did not see that in myself.

And by the way, what a powerful picture of mentoring; not only do people choose to pour into one another, they have the ability to see further into you than you can see yourself. She saw that in me. She spoke truth into me. And she gave me the gift to see that and speak that into others.

My assistant superintendent continued, "You are able to clearly see where we are, and where we could be . . . and you bring people together to help the entire organization get from one place to another." Wow . . .

This was a turning point, and vision was at the crux of it all. Once I expanded my personal vision of what could be, my mindset shifted, and all of a sudden what I thought wasn't even on the table, was. And as I realized what professional vision really is as a leader of an organization, I also realized that I had it. This made me able to approach what once seemed unapproachable.

As I find myself in seasons where my 95 percent looks distant, I try to ground myself in my personal vision as well as in our organization's shared vision. As I began to recognize my misconceptions about vision and reframe my thoughts around what vision really is and why it is important, it changed my trajectory both personally and professionally. So how do you lead from vision?

PRACTICAL TRUTHS TO POWERFULLY LEAD WITH VISION

Vision Is What Could Be

Vision is not just some foggy, hard to define, mystical kind of concept. Vision is simply being able to see what could be. Sometimes you will be the conduit bringing people together to share their greatest hopes and dreams together to find their vision. In fact, the clearer the vision, the more powerful it will become. As Simon Sinek shared in *Leaders Eat Last*, "Short- or long-term, the clearer we can see what we are setting out to achieve, the more likely we are to achieve it."[3]

Each year we spend time during our new-to-district orientation introducing our new staff, and I ask each of them the same question: Why Gunter ISD? When they get done, they have more clearly

---

3   Simon Sinek, *Leaders Eat Last: Why Some Teams Pull Together and Others Don't* (New York: Penguin, 2014).

articulated the culture, values, and beliefs of our district than I ever could.[4] People know what Gunter is about; they believe in our shared beliefs, and they feel our culture. Jon Gordon talks about this kind of culture in *The Power of Positive Leadership*. He notes, "You can't just create a culture where people hear about what's important. You must create a culture where people feel what's important. You must create a culture where people don't just hear your talk but rather they *feel* your walk."[5]

VISION SHOULD BE SO CLEAR THAT IT DOESN'T NEED A SLOGAN FOR PEOPLE TO MEMORIZE; THEY JUST KNOW WHAT YOU'RE ABOUT.

Vision Is More than Future Focused

Part of vision is absolutely the ability to see into the *future*, to help the organization or yourself see what could be. Sinek wrote about former CEOs now having a "sober clarity" that we wish they'd possessed while they were leading. He said, "I understand we all have 20/20 hindsight, but don't we pay these leaders for their vision and foresight?" A key aspect of vision is being able to see into the future, and as Dr. John

---

4   Every child is unique and is valued and cared for; high expectations and work are critical for success; learning is broader than the state standards, and the goal is to develop not only lifelong learners but to teach citizenship and high character, etc: www.gunterisd.org/strategicplan.

5   Jon Gordon, *The Power of Positive Leadership* (New York: Wiley, 2017).

Horn with the Schlechty Center would add, "The higher up in the organization you go, the further out your vision needs to be."[6]

But sometimes we look at vision as being *solely future-focused*. I think a big part of vision is being able to see it *all*. It is having a clear understanding and perspective of the *past*; about where you've come from, the successes and failures within that, and the legacy that needs to be cherished from that. It's about seeing where you are in the *present* and understanding where you are in the context of others *around* you. And the context includes seeing the good, the bad, and the ugly. Having vision does not mean the path will be clear; it simply means being able to see the path, including every opportunity and every obstacle in your way. Vision is the ability to *see* both the big picture from thirty thousand feet and the details right in front of you—the past, the present, and the future, and most importantly, the path from where you are to where you want to be.

Vision is big picture and laser focus. Gordon talks about using both a telescope and microscope in our leadership: "The telescope helps you and your team keep your eyes on the vision, North Star, and big picture. The microscope helps you zoom-focus on the things you must do in the short term to realize the vision in your telescope."[7] As leaders we must simultaneously keep our eyes on the big picture *and* pay attention to the acute actions that must happen for our vision to be realized.

Vision is also never-ending. There is no moment of arrival. I love the video by John Spencer called *Empower: What Happens When Students Own Their Learning*.[8] It's a simple video that notes that we often talk about moving from compliance to engagement (a decades-long push for educators) and beautifully walks you through a complete

---

6   The Schlechty Center was founded by Phil Schlechty and is focused on working with schools to further a culture of engagement through designing meaningful learning for students: https://www.schlechtycenter.org.

7   Jon Gordon, *The Power of Positive Leadership* (New York: Wiley, 2017).

8   John Spencer, "The Shift from Engaging Students to Empowering Learners," June 9, 2017, https://www.youtube.com/watch?v=BYBJQ5rIFjA.

paradigm shift, recognizing that "if we want students to be creative, self-directed learners, we need to move beyond student engagement and into empowerment." He describes the shift from making the subject interesting to tapping into student interests, from taking assessments to assessing your own learning, from teachers asking all the questions to students asking their own questions. We have come so far in the realm of teaching and learning, shifting from a system of compliance to one of engagement. But when Spencer talks about the power in shifting from mere engagement to empowerment, it helped me realize that as we continue to refine the craft of teaching and learning, there will always be a better way. We will never arrive. The same is true for our vision: we will never fully arrive. As leaders, our vision is continually being refined and refocused just as the world around us and the students in front of us continue to change and exhibit different needs.

VISION IS THE ABILITY TO SEE BOTH THE BIG PICTURE FROM THIRTY THOUSAND FEET AND THE DETAILS RIGHT IN FRONT OF YOU. THE PAST, THE PRESENT, AND THE FUTURE. AND MOST IMPORTANTLY, THE PATH FROM WHERE YOU ARE TO WHERE YOU WANT TO BE.

Vision Is Not a Solitary Creation

Leaders don't own the market when it comes to vision; everyone has great hopes and dreams. Vision truly comes to life when people share those hopes and dreams and together forge aspirations of where the organization can and should go. Our job as leaders is to bring diverse voices into the process, to push people to broaden their mindsets about what could be, and to open our minds and hearts to hear the desires of the group.

VISION TRULY COMES TO LIFE WHEN PEOPLE SHARE THEIR HOPES AND DREAMS AND TOGETHER FORGE ASPIRATIONS OF WHERE THE ORGANIZATION CAN AND SHOULD GO.

The strategic planning process for my district was incredible. And that was not only because we brought in two professional strategic planning facilitators who had mastered bringing people together to share a collective voice about their aspirations, but because of the collective group itself. David Weinberger, author of *Too Big to Know*, shared that "the smartest person in the room is the room."[9] And when it comes to vision, you need to make sure that your room is large enough to collect the unique thoughts and perspectives of your entire school community. That only happens when you are intentional about the design of those activities in order to ensure that *all* voices are heard, not just the most dominant voice. The magic is not in a pretty piece of paper or a well-worded statement, or whatever result or product that comes out of it; the magic happens through the rich conversations generated in the process itself.

---

9   David Weinberger, *Too Big to Know: Rethinking Knowledge Now That the Facts Aren't the Facts, Experts Are Everywhere, and the Smartest Person in the Room Is the Room* (New York: Basic Books, 2014).

DIVERSITY OF THOUGHT ONLY HAPPENS WHEN YOU ARE INTENTIONAL ABOUT THE DESIGN OF ACTIVITIES TO ENSURE THAT ALL VOICES ARE HEARD. THE MAGIC IS NOT THE PRETTY PIECE OF PAPER OR WELL-WORDED STATEMENT; **THE MAGIC HAPPENS THROUGH THE RICH CONVERSATIONS GENERATED IN THE PROCESS ITSELF.**

Vision is also not reserved for adults. Sometimes the vision of your school organization comes directly from its students. We have had students involved in our strategic planning process from the beginning, as part of our initial strategic planning teams, community forums, and action teams, and through surveys and committees like our high school principal's student advisory team. As our school board was reading through the whole collection of data received from our school community survey, we saw that one of our graduates had responded that his greatest hope was that ours would continue to be an exceptional school that developed great people who better the world. The vision statement of Gunter ISD later came to be *an exceptional school system that develops great people who better the world.* Student voice matters.

Vision Alone Is Not Enough

Having vision is only helpful when there is capacity to bring the vision to life. Jack Welch, the long-time CEO of GE, noted that "good business leaders create a vision, articulate the vision, passionately own the vision, and relentlessly drive it to completion."[10] One of the most frustrating aspects of being part of an organization is to have a leader that has a vision but an organization that is incapable of achieving it. As leaders, vision is important, but we must ensure that we gather people around us who can bring the vision to life. Vision must be created, communicated, cared for by its people, and brought to completion.

Vision Is Personal

While vision is important for organizations, having a personal vision is equally important. We need to continually envision what our life could be and analyze whether we are taking steps toward those aspirations. Marianne Williamson shared that "our deepest fear is not that we are inadequate. Our deepest fear is that we are powerful beyond measure. It is our light, not our darkness, that most frightens us."[11]

Personal vision is important because when we are not mindful of what could be, we will bury our greatest hopes and dreams under the guise of busyness or even impossibility—when sometimes, it's not about ability, it's about *our fear of the possibility*. The power of personal vision is in pushing yourself to think about what your strengths are, where your joy is, what the ideal life would look like, and what changes need to be made in order to pursue that path—and then going for it!

Conclusion

Sometimes our 5 percent is happening because we are floundering due to a lack of clear vision. I shared earlier about the financial crisis my district was facing when I took on the superintendency. The truth is, the easiest time to lead from a vision perspective was those first two years. I absolutely knew where my focus needed to be and

---

10 Jack Welch, quoted by Noel Tichy and Ram Charan in "Speed, Simplicity, Self-Confidence: An Interview with Jack Welch," *Harvard Business Review*, September-October 1989, https://hbr.org/1989/09/speed-simplicity-self-confidence-an-interview-with-jack-welch.

11 Marianne Williamson, *A Return to Love: Reflections on the Principles of a Course in Miracles* (New York: HarperCollins, 1992).

what decisions needed to be made in year one, and then learned to live with the decisions we made in year two. But in years three and four, I found myself anxious, almost floundering, because my vision was not clear. We had accomplished what we set out to do financially or were at least on the road to financial recovery, and as a district, we were very successful academically and in our extracurricular programs as well. *Vision is galvanized through crisis, but in times of relative success and comfort, vision must be sought consciously and aggressively.* I am thankful that our district started our strategic planning process to determine the future for our schools and students together, but that in-between season was challenging.

WHEN WE ARE NOT MINDFUL OF OUR PERSONAL VISION, WE CAN BURY OUR HOPES AND DREAMS UNDER THE GUISE OF BUSYNESS OR EVEN IMPOSSIBILITY. WHEN IT'S NOT ABOUT ABILITY, IT'S ABOUT OUR FEAR OF THE POSSIBILITY.

Benjamin Franklin used to ask this powerful question: "What has become clear to you since we last met?" If we are going to be the best versions of ourselves and serve our families and organizations well, we must have clarity around what we want to do and who we want to be. Be bold! There is great vision within all of us—around what we want to do and who we want to be. But it takes being *mindful* about and *intentional* in creating our vision, bringing people together to embody our vision, and then living it out—in big ways and small ways . . . Every. Single. Day.

THERE IS GREAT VISION WITHIN EACH OF US—AROUND WHAT WE WANT TO DO AND WHO WE WANT TO BE. WE MUST BE MINDFUL AND INTENTIONAL IN LIVING IT OUT IN BIG WAYS AND SMALL WAYS . . . EVERY SINGLE DAY.

5 TIPS TO THRIVE

1   Put it on the table. All of it. Every possibility. No matter how far-fetched. Erase the box you are subconsciously drawing around your possibilities and just let yourself dream.

2   Spend time thinking through your personal vision statement. Why do you do what you do? What really inspires you? Are you living out your personal vision?

3   Just like building a shared vision in an organization, consider involving those you trust when building your personal vision. What strengths do they see in you? What can you do that no one else can do?

4   Think of three small things that could move you toward where you really want to go. Then think of three more things to add to that list. Now choose one and do it!

5   Think about stretching your professional network to include people who will challenge your thinking. Surround yourself with some new voices and ideas.

Vision without action is merely a dream. Action without vision just passes the time. Vision with action can change the world. ★
—Joel A. Barker

Lead from Vision

Thrive Through the Five by Jill M. Siler

Vision Is What Could Be

Vision Is More than Future-Focused

The higher up in the organization you go, the further out your vision needs to be

PRESENT · FUTURE · PAST

Past · Future

Vision Is Personal

Mindful of what could be

Vision Alone Is Not Enough

created → Vision must be... ← communicated
↓
VISION
cared for by its people

Vision Is Not a Solitary Creation

vision comes to life when people SHARE

Vision is galvanized through crisis, but in times of relative success and comfort, vision must be sought aggressively.

Sketchnote by Amelia Buchanan
@edtech_amelia

FRAMEWORK TO THRIVE: VISION

How does your current path compare to where you thought you'd be ten to fifteen years ago?	*What changed in your personal or professional vision to allow you to grow?*

Is your vision big enough, or have you drawn a small box within the huge expanse of what could be?

How are you living within your vision and taking steps to bring it to fruition?

How does understanding our need to lead from vision help you think about thriving in the 5 percent?

TWELVE

TAKE THE NEXT BEST STEP

*Sometimes the smallest step in the right
direction ends up being the biggest step of your
life. Tiptoe if you must, but take a step.*

—NAEEM CALLAWAY

At the beginning of last year, I went to our state's education leadership conference and to the women's leadership conference. I attended these conferences back-to-back, just as I've done in years past. I presented at both, just as I've done in years past. Every year these conferences are inspiring: one brings five thousand-plus leaders from across Texas to share how they are impacting the lives of students each and every day. The other brings women who are leading at all levels together to empower and inspire one another.[1]

But last year something was different; something had changed. That was a watershed week for me. I shared in an earlier chapter that during that time I went to my old church in Austin and heard a message that absolutely grabbed my soul.[2] It was out of Deuteronomy, and the text was "you've stayed at the mountain long enough." So

---

1   The Texas Association of School Administrators (TASA) Midwinter Conference: https://tasamidwinter.org/. The Texas Council of Women School Executives (TCWSE): https://tcwse.org/.

2   Keith Pate, "Illuminate: A Spiritual Foundation That Lasts," message shared at New Hope First Baptist Church, Cedar Park, TX, https://vimeo.com/313878959.

many thoughts and hopes and dreams that had been locked away for longer than I can remember were set free in my mind—and there was no turning back. It was a turning point.

But here's the thing: In that moment, in that watershed week, I didn't hear anything *specific* about what that would mean, what that would look like, what was to come. I didn't know that in the year that followed I would have the opportunity to do my first TED-like talk at a women's leadership conference. I didn't know that I was going to walk away from that event inspired to start a blog that soon would have over twelve thousand views. I didn't realize that I would have the opportunity to have my first article published in the national school leadership magazine. I didn't know I would have the opportunity to lead our state's Aspiring Superintendent Academy with over 170 leaders. I didn't know that I would be inspired to write a book, put together a proposal, get a contract, and turn in a complete manuscript that same year. And I certainly didn't know that I would then be asked to keynote the very conference that had started the trajectory of that extraordinary year!

Let me be clear: I didn't have an inkling that any of those things would happen that year.

But that's what we want sometimes. We feel inspired, we feel a call, and we think we should just leap from point A to point Z in one fell swoop. And when we can't, we get stuck.

Oswald Chambers said, "God engineers our circumstances . . . All we have to do is follow where He places us. The majority of us are busy trying to place ourselves."[3] Just one more time for those in the back: "the majority of us are busy trying to place ourselves."

All of that time and energy I've spent wondering and questioning: Am I where I'm supposed to be? Am I still effective here? Would another leader better serve this district? How will I know if I'm supposed to move somewhere else? What does my future hold?

---

3   Oswald Chambers, *The Love of God: An Intimate Look at the Father-Heart of God* (New York: Discovery House, 1988).

Just stop. Stop trying to place yourself, and be faithful to what is before you.

STOP TRYING TO PLACE YOURSELF. JUST BE FAITHFUL TO WHAT IS BEFORE YOU.

For so long I felt that the only way I could broaden my leadership or have a greater impact on others would be to leave this beautiful community in which I live and serve. And I struggled between my (and my family's) desire to stay here and the urge to lead in a broader way. The turning point came that Sunday morning, when I realized that I didn't have to *leave* in order to *lead* in the way that I felt like I was—and am—being called to.

I absolutely love the thousand students in the district I serve, but I am also deeply passionate about the 5.4 million students across our great state. And if there is a way that I can pour into other leaders and increase their impact on kids and teachers while still doing the work I love in this community in which I feel called to serve, you better believe I'm all in.

What came next was the question of whether I was willing to step out of my comfort zone, to be bold and brave, and to expand my leadership in a broader way. And once my answer was yes, it became a series of tiny steps: some exciting and some extremely uncomfortable. Contrary to popular belief, big things don't always happen with a leap; big things can happen when we continue to take the next best step, over and over again.

My first step was to give voice to my big thoughts and dreams. One of my sister superintendents and best friends was the first person to whom I uttered the very scary words "I want to write a book." She responded with an enthusiasm I will forever cherish. Yet as soon as those words escaped my soul, fear and doubt began to bubble up, and I added this caveat that I was thinking about partnering with a distinguished gentleman who was much more experienced than I was. I am so thankful that my friend replied, "Absolutely not." You see, she saw that those words were not coming from a place of desire for collaboration, but from a place of fear. She wanted to make perfectly clear that I was absolutely enough to do this thing that had been laid on my heart. Just as we are all enough to do the things that have been laid on our hearts.

That small, bold step launched a whole series of next best steps. I applied to share a TED-like talk at a women's conference. That event inspired me, both hearing the speakers and having the opportunity to speak myself, and I realized I wanted to share my thoughts on a broader scale. I looked up a few bloggers and learned what platform they used, started my own website, and began to blog. I didn't even know what to write about in the beginning, so my first five posts were the text of that speech broken up into smaller blogs, giving me thirty days to find my voice. My formula was simple: Be authentic and speak truth. Be thoughtful, purposeful, and practical. Encourage and empower others.

I continued to set small goals. I set aside three hours a week to write. I set a goal to hit Publish every other week to share thoughts with my professional learning networks. I knew nothing about the process of writing a book, so I set a summer goal of contacting ten authors. I sent direct messages on Twitter and LinkedIn. I found email addresses and reached out to writers at their places of work and enjoyed gracious conversation after gracious conversation. Some shared how they put together their book proposals; others shared what to look for in publishers and contracts; one even showed me what I needed to be writing about (which was very different from what I thought I would be writing about). I sent introductory emails to publishers with samples of my writing and asked for an opportunity to visit.

I landed a conversation with Dave Burgess and DBC Inc. and was impressed with their clear vision and support of thought leaders in the field. I committed to Dave in that July conversation that I would put together a book proposal within two months. (Clearly I am an idiot. What school leader has time in August and September to write a book proposal?) My husband I looked at our calendars and found one weekend that was from the heavens, one weekend that was free from kids' sporting events, district events—you name it. I wanted to give myself the best shot to do this, and so I even took off one day of work to connect to that weekend. But as the days led up to the day I was going to take off for this long weekend I was going to write, my anxiety began to build. By the time that Friday morning came, I was beside myself, sick. My husband came in and asked what was wrong, and I began to share my fears: What if I can't do this? What I have nothing to write about? What if I have nothing to say? And (in a way that explains why we happily celebrated our twentieth anniversary this year) he responded, "Jill, if it doesn't work, if you don't have anything to say . . . don't worry about it. Go get a massage, a pedicure—this is the first day off you've taken in months!" I went and wrote and ten hours later saw this beautiful frame of what I hope will help others lead through the most challenging days. In the weeks to come, I got up the courage to hit Send, and a contract arrived a few weeks later.

I say all that to say this: people who saw the events in the past twelve months of my life were amazed that I was able to do this "big thing" in writing a book.

But I look back at this past twelve months and don't see a big thing.

I see one small step, followed by one small goal, followed by one more small but bold thing that put me on the trajectory to where I felt called, followed by one more act of being faithful to what was before me.

The end result is huge, but the journey to get there did not consist of big leaps. It was one small step—over and over and over again.

Sometimes our 5 percent is the struggle we feel due to the gap between where we are and where we want to be. When we redirect our focus away from the chasm before us and just focus on the very next best step in front of us, we can make significant gains on our dreams.

BIG THINGS DON'T ALWAYS HAPPEN WITH A LEAP. BIG THINGS HAPPEN WHEN WE TAKE THE NEXT BEST STEP . . . OVER AND OVER AND OVER AGAIN.

PRACTICAL TRUTHS TO POWERFULLY LEAD YOUR NEXT BEST STEP

It's Time to Leave the Mountain of Comfort

We are a people who enjoy comfort. Yet comfort is not the thing that will bring us to the place of "what could be" in our lives. The author Daniel Pink discusses how "we need a place of productive discomfort." He shares in *Drive* that "If you're too comfortable, you're not productive. And if you're too uncomfortable, you're not productive."[4] We need to reassess every area of our life—from our professional work to our personal finances to our physical health to our emotional and spiritual well-being, and discern whether we're comfortable or in a state of panic or in that sweet spot of uncomfortable and growing. Our 5 percent seasons could be coming from merely being too comfortable or from living in a state of panic and high stress for too long.

So how do you do that? You just start. Just one small, bold step after another. A funny thing happens when you start doing that . . . You find that soon you just can't stop. Have you ever been playing with a paper clip and realized you completely opened it up? Knowing that you still need to use it, you try to bend it back together again, but it doesn't ever look the same. It has been changed by your movement.

---

4   Daniel Pink, *Drive: The Surprising Truth About What Motivates Us* (New York: Riverhead, 2009).

In the same way, when you begin to take small, bold steps out of your comfort zone, you are no longer the person you once were—and you can't ever go back.

ONCE YOU TAKE SMALL, BOLD STEPS OUT OF YOUR COMFORT ZONE, YOU ARE NO LONGER THE PERSON YOU ONCE WERE, AND YOU CAN'T EVER GO BACK.

Stop Trying to Place Yourself

Author Brianna Wiest wrote a piece about this notion of forcing a particular outcome. It was an article that really challenged my beliefs, as her tag line was "follow the 'law of least effort' to do more of what works." I think my struggle with it was "least effort," but she made a compelling argument:

> Success starts with us. Our interests, skills, and passions; our trauma and our grievances; the chips on our shoulders and the dreams in our hearts are not random. The place where they intersect is our calling, and it is wholly and completely unique to each of us. We don't have to force it. We don't have to compete for it. We simply have to respond to it, start showing up to it, and then, like the sand in our palms, learn to loosen our grip, and allow it to be.[5]

---

5   Brianna Wiest, "When You Attempt to Force an Outcome, the Universe Will Resist," Forge, March 17, 2019, https://forge.medium.com/the-law-of-least -effort-is-the-success-secret-nobody-talks-about-c713eeab8ade.

Sometimes we get so fixated on where we *think* we should be that we lose sight of the beauty of what we're actually learning and doing, and how we're growing exactly where we are.

SOMETIMES WE GET SO FIXATED ON WHERE WE THINK WE SHOULD BE THAT WE LOSE SIGHT OF THE BEAUTY OF WHAT WE'RE ACTUALLY LEARNING AND HOW WE'RE GROWING EXACTLY WHERE WE ARE.

Give Voice to Your Big Thoughts and Dreams

I generally haven't struggled with sharing my goals with others— things like when I wanted to move into a leadership position or get my master's or doctorate. Those were expected moves in the context of what I was doing at the time. But some steps that I have taken came with as much doubt and fear as exhilaration and passion—steps like moving into the superintendency or writing this book. These were goals and dreams I really struggled to talk about with others for a myriad of reasons, most likely because of the inherent level of risk in reaching them. Jack Canfield, the author of *Chicken Soup for the Soul*, spoke directly to this as he noted:

> An individual's goals are very personal. In fact, a well thought out goal hints at the person's vulnerability and deepest desires. Not only do goals reflect a person's desires, goals also have the incredible power to change a person's life—if executed well of course.[6]

6   Jack Canfield, "The Power of Sharing Your Goals with Others," https://www.jackcanfield.com/blog/goal-sharing/.

Big dreams are very personal indeed, and I appreciate how he noted that they unveil a depth of vulnerability we're not often comfortable revealing. He offered two reasons that sharing these deepest desires can be immeasurably powerful. First, through articulating these thoughts with others, we gain clarity. I was listening to NPR's *How I Built This* as founder David Neeleman stated that before he launched the successful JetBlue airline, he had to find his reason for being: "I would never start an airline or take over an airline that I thought didn't have a reason for being."[7] He saw a clear need in that the major carriers offered high costs and poor customer service, and he launched JetBlue as a "customer service company that flies airplanes."[8]

In the same way, we have to have clarity in what we are doing and why we are doing it. What is our reason for being in what we are trying to achieve?

Canfield also notes that sharing goals with others can be powerful because it provides accountability. When we wish for something or privately write about something we want, there is little skin in the game. Stating our dreams to others, however, inherently makes us more accountable. It brings what was private into the public, it allows others to invest in our progress, and heightens expectations. I continued writing this book in the weeks I waited to see if my proposal would be accepted. By the time I received a contract and shared about it publicly, I was far enough along to be confident in my now very public goals.

Sharing goals can be scary, but giving voice to your big hopes and dreams is a necessary step to truly achieving "what could be" in your life.

---

7   David Neeleman, "Jet Blue Airways," *How I Built This*, February 1, 2019, https://www.npr.org/2019/02/01/690686584/jetblue-airways-david-neeleman.

8   Benjamin Zhang, "JetBlue's Founder Reveals Tips for Success in the Airline Business," Business Insider, September 29, 2018, https://www.businessinsider.com/jetblue-azul-founder-david-neeleman-explains-secret-to-success-in-airlines-2018-9.

Focus on Small Steps

The big dream is important and powerful. But the way to achieve the dream isn't to dream or to focus on the big dream. Jon Acuff, author of *Finish: Give Yourself the Gift of Done*, noted that:

> The reality is when you say, "Aim for the moon, because even if you fail, you'll land amongst the stars." That's not how life works. People quit when they fail. The problem is we judge on a pass/fail scale, so if I want to lose ten pounds and I lose eight, I failed by two and I give up. So the idea of having this crazy goal that's your main goal just cripples people from the beginning.[9]

James Clear, author of *Atomic Habits*, notes: "Too often we convince ourselves that massive success requires massive action." He talks about making small, atomic, changes in our behaviors that will ultimately result in huge successes: "Meanwhile, improving by one percent isn't particularly notable—sometimes it isn't even noticeable—but it can be far more meaningful, especially in the long run." Clear notes that we "should be far more concerned with our current trajectory than with our current results."[10] That's why there is power in taking the next best step.

Conclusion

The 5 percent can come from staying at our "mountain of comfort" too long, and we need to find our voice to share our dreams and then muster the courage to step boldly away from the known. Or our difficulties may stem from a deep yearning to be at a different phase of our life, yet we're caught in the gap and need to remember to just focus on the small step in front of us. When we take small steps that are in alignment with our huge dream, we will continue to make progress, gain confidence, and ultimately step into our calling!

9 Jon Acuff, *Finish: Give Yourself the Gift of Done* (New York: Portfolio, 2018).

10 James Clear, *Atomic Habits: An Easy & Proven Way to Build Good Habits & Break Bad Ones* (New York: Avery, 2018).

5 TIPS TO THRIVE

1 Don't get lost in mapping a path to where you want to be. Just determine the next best step, no matter how small, and take it. Then do it again (and again and again).

2 Choose one person you know and trust to share your big dream with. Don't pull back or second-guess or let your fear take away from your dreams.

3 Not to steal Nike's thunder, but "just do it." That conference you've been thinking about presenting at, that great idea you've been thinking about sharing with your team, that creative thing you'd like to give yourself time and space for . . . just do it.

4 Look up. In the midst of all that we do, lift your head and see the beauty in what you've done and in just being.

5 Sometimes your next step happens in the positioning. Instead of looking at what's to come, knock it out of the park *today*. The greatness you pour into the everyday work will position you for tomorrow.

Sometimes the smallest step in the right direction ends up being the biggest step of your life. Tiptoe if you must, but take a step.
~ Naeem Callaway

Take the Next Best Step

Thrive Through the Five by Jill M. Siler

LEVEL UP It's Time to Leave the Mountain of Comfort

LEVEL UP Stop Trying to Place Yourself

"Headed towards what should be"

sometimes we get so fixated on where we think we should be that we lose sight of the beauty

WHERE WE THINK WE SHOULD BE

LEVEL UP Give Voice to Your Big Thoughts and Dreams

LEVEL UP Focus on Small Steps

HOPES
DREAMS
SHARE GOALS WITH OTHERS
provides accountability

make progress
gain confidence

The end result is huge, but the journey to get there rarely consists of big leaps. It is one small step... over and over again.

Sketchnote by Amelia Buchanan
@edtech_amelia

FRAMEWORK TO THRIVE: TAKE THE NEXT BEST STEP

What mountain of comfort have you been at too long?	*What is holding you back from taking one small but bold step forward?*
What big hopes and dreams do you need to give voice to?	*Who can you share those with that will edify, challenge, and inspire you?*

How does the thought of just taking the next best step help you think about thriving in the 5 percent?

THIRTEEN

THIS TOO SHALL PASS

Nothing lasts forever—not even your troubles.
—ARNOLD H. GLASOW

There are four words that sustain me through my 5 percent days, weeks, and seasons. As a woman of faith, I wish I could say they are from deep spiritual truth or even some profound philosophical tenet. But really, the words I cling to are *this too shall pass*. Originally a Persian adage from the early nineteenth century, these words have been invoked for centuries to depict the ebb and flow of life. Abraham Lincoln used these words as well, in the year leading up to his election as president:

> It is said an Eastern monarch once charged his wise men to invent him a sentence, to be ever in view, and which should be true and appropriate in all times and situations. They presented him the words: "And this, too, shall pass away." How much it expresses! How chastening in the hour of pride! How consoling in the depths of affliction![1]

I shared earlier that during the first eighteen months of the superintendency, I had several moments where I contemplated getting out. And I think one of the biggest reasons for my angst and discomfort

---

1 Abraham Lincoln's Speech to the Wisconsin State Agricultural Society (1859), http://www.abrahamlincolnonline.org/lincoln/speeches/fair.htm.

is that I didn't understand this truth—that this too shall pass. Almost everything is a little better in the morning—and the next morning, and the next week, and the next week after that.

This is more than a mindset or an optimistic hope. It is the reality: whatever situation we are facing will get better. The speed at which it improves and the degree to which it improves are, of course, dependent on the situation itself. There are some tragedies where it is truly weeks and months before there is healing and recovery. But far more often, our 5 percent issues are from the challenging things that pop up at surprising moments to cause us temporary grief and heartache. When we face these moments, we feel the hopelessness will last forever—but it won't. A friend recently reminded me of the saying that "things are never as bad as they seem, nor as good as they feel." When I have a 5 percent day, or week, or season, I remember that things will get better.

What do you do during the moments you're waiting for it to pass? During those days where you wish you could find a rock and crawl under it? My suggestion is simply to give yourself some grace. Feel the feelings—just for a little bit. And then get on to the work at hand. This too shall pass.

PRACTICAL TRUTHS TO POWERFULLY LEAD TO ALLOW TIME TO HEAL

Find Solace

One of the worst parts about dealing with the 5 percent is managing our feelings around challenging aspects of our work. More often than not, I can think through the solutions or find next best steps in any situation. But somehow, knowing how to improve something in the future doesn't remove the feelings of grief, dread, frustration, hurt, embarrassment, anger, and regret that cause pain now. *But our leadership is needed beyond the one issue that is causing heartache,* so we must find solace to restore our hearts and minds to lead another day. That looks different for everyone. For me, solace is in spending time with my family, talking with a friend or colleague, reading a book, watching a movie or writing, spending time in prayer and reflection, working out, and sleeping.

Finding comfort can absolutely mean doing joyful things to keep your mind off of the stress at hand. Everything I mentioned above truly does help—sometimes. But sometimes, solace is found only after delving into the feelings until we find peace.

I consider myself someone who has a high threshold for stress and pressure. This is coupled with a healthy dose of confidence and a strong sense of self. I share this with you so that you'll understand the irony that I also struggle with anxiety. It is not an everyday thing—it comes and goes like an unwelcome cold. I have been known to become incredibly anxious before speaking events, contentious meetings, and other events that can be anxiety inducing. And I can become anxious at totally normal events for no apparent reason. I have studied for years to find the pattern: Is it the size of the crowd, how well I know the crowd, how much or how little I am prepared, how important the event is, how contentious the situation is? I've got nothing. And if you've ever struggled with anxiety, you'll understand that the anxiety *around* whether you're going to experience anxiety is almost as bad as the anxiety itself (not quite, but a close second).

A few years back, I attended a meeting with all of the area superintendents in my athletic district over a case of whether to grant eligibility to an athlete who had recently moved into our school district. These superintendents were close colleagues—I saw them weekly. I have led countless meetings with them. They know me as a strong and confident leader. All I had to do was overview the steps we had taken to ensure this student moved here on his own without contact from our coaches or athletes. My notes were well-prepared, and there was not an ounce of worry about our steps in the process. Yet when it came time for me to speak, I . . . couldn't. My heart was pounding so hard I was sure people could see it; my hands were shaking, and I couldn't breathe. I took a sip of water, tried to breathe deeply, and still couldn't get it together. I finally eked out a "Go ahead and review my notes, and then I'll hit the high points in just a minute." Nice save, but not everyone in the audience had notes— which led to a long period of people just staring at me.

It was not the first time. But it was the time that prompted me to get help.[2] I started a relationship with an amazing counselor I continue to see during particularly stressful seasons. She has helped me understand that sometimes personal life events and stress can impact our emotional state. So while that particular athletic meeting had no grounds for the anxiety, the five other major events happening in my personal life at that time did. She also taught me practical strategies for the next time I faced the impact of anxiety in my personal and professional life. These include everything from breathing exercises to strategies to ground my physical reaction in the midst of anxiety to planning purposeful activities while public speaking that will allow me to catch my breath (literally).

There was one specific strategy she encouraged that I will never forget. She recommended that I "sit in those feelings." I almost laughed at her: "Are you *kidding* me? That is the last thing I want to do." But she continued, saying that only once you are willing to process those feelings and get to the bottom of whatever is causing you angst, will you be able to heal and find peace.

It's not that those moments have never happened again; they have. It's not that I have found the magical formula for when they happen; I have not. It is that I now understand that in some situations, going to a movie or spending time with friends won't bring peace—it simply prolongs the hurt until I spend time working through those feelings. We must be whole ourselves in order to pour into others, so we must use our time to find solace.

---

2   There are so many incredible support resources out there. A great place to start is NAMI (National Alliance on Mental Illness): www.nami.org.

Let Time Work for You

One of the things that gave me freedom in leadership was realizing that many decisions do not need to be made in the moment. In fact, sometimes it is better to walk away, let it sit, and come back to it. Chapter 5 talked about the importance of taking our time on decisions that matter. Sometimes time works out the situation for us. When we give a situation some air, the parties involved have some space to reflect and reconvene, and by the time we come back to it, the situation is closer to resolution. The art of leadership is discerning which situations need immediate attention and action and which decisions would be assisted by some time and space.

> MANY DECISIONS DO NOT NEED TO BE MADE IN THE MOMENT. THE ART OF LEADERSHIP IS DISCERNING WHICH SITUATIONS NEED IMMEDIATE ATTENTION AND WHICH DECISIONS COULD BE IMPROVED WITH SOME TIME AND SPACE.

In the same respect, make sure your time works *for* you. Shelley Burgess and Beth Houf talk about the critical importance of how we spend our time. They note, "If you want to transform what is happening in your school or district, you have to immerse yourself in the work that has the highest impact on increasing student learning and building a rich, powerful, and positive culture."

Burgess and Houf share a great time-management activity for leaders, where you list all of the activities you do, rate them as having high or low impact, and then rearrange them by what takes most of your time. This helped my leadership team realize that some of their lowest-impact work was taking up the majority of their time. We have to be intentional with our most precious resources—ourselves and our time—and look at everyone in the organization to see if there are other people whose skills could be utilized to accomplish things in a better way.

Be Faithful in the Little Things

In those moments when I'm waiting for a 5 percent season to pass, I have to remember to be faithful in the little things. There are seasons for each of us where we feel we're not quite where we want to be, and during those times it's especially important to be faithful in the little things. You may not be in the leadership position you'd ultimately like to be in. But I would say to you: it doesn't matter. Lead anyway. Your ability to lead is not defined or confined by your role, title, or position. Every day find ways to make everything and everyone around you better!

YOUR ABILITY TO LEAD IS NOT DEFINED OR CONFINED BY YOUR ROLE, TITLE, OR POSITION. EVERY DAY FIND WAYS TO MAKE EVERYTHING AND EVERYONE AROUND YOU BETTER!

At one point in my leadership journey, I desperately wanted to be at the next step. There was someone in that position (whom I adored) and they were going to retire . . . someday. My professional plan was to wait for them to retire . . . someday. By the way, this is not a plan I would recommend to anyone. There were times when it was frustrating, but I continued to find ways to allow my leadership to grow, and I'm so thankful I had people around me who helped me do the same.

During that time, my superintendent met with me and shared that they were reshaping my roles and responsibilities—and I was excited! Until I found out I was going to become the Level II grievance hearing officer for our district. Friends, there are a lot of incredible things that people can ordain you with. Becoming a Level II grievance officer is *not* one of them.

Comedian Heather Land does funny sixty-second video clips from her car that all end with this statement: "I ain't doin it." Her rants all include this classic line toward the end: "I would rather. . ."[3] And they are audacious things like "I would rather stick ten needles in my eyes than get up to do a CrossFit workout" or "I would rather dance the two-step on hot coals than eat out on Valentine's Day by myself."

Let me just tell you: I would rather do just about anything than lead a Level II grievance hearing.

But I did it anyway. And I did it well. And I learned so much in the process. I learned how to really listen and help find the root cause of a concerned parent. I learned how to de-escalate contentious situations. I learned how to work together to find common ground. I was faithful in the little things that have served me so well ever since. When we are faithful in our journey—even when it feels like our work is that of a mustard seed—success will follow.

WHEN WE ARE FAITHFUL IN OUR JOURNEY—EVEN WHEN IT FEELS LIKE OUR WORK IS THAT OF A MUSTARD SEED—SUCCESS WILL FOLLOW.

3   You can check out Heather Land at: www.heatherlandofficial.com.

Our softball team enjoyed a recent victory.[4] It wasn't just any win, it was a win that finished an undefeated 12–0 season in district play, a win that solidified the district championship, and a win that marked the end of a long five-year stretch where we hadn't even made the playoffs. As the athletic director, principal, and I walked out onto the field, district trophy in hand, we asked if we could interrupt the team's huddle. The coach politely told us no. You see, they weren't quite finished yet.

As family and friends started to gather around, they proceeded to enter into a time of accountability—each player taking responsibility for things they could have done better—and then finished with shout-outs, with players highlighting exceptional things their teammates had done. Their team meeting ended, and the celebration commenced. What I walked away with that night was confirmation that this team was absolutely committed to the little things.

Life isn't about the immediate win. It's about the long-term goal—and not sacrificing the learning that happens along the way, even in the wins. And to achieve that long-term goal, we must remain faithful in the little things.

No. Matter. What.

LIFE ISN'T ABOUT THE IMMEDIATE WIN. IT'S ABOUT THE LONG-TERM GOAL—AND NOT SACRIFICING THE LEARNING THAT HAPPENS ALONG THE WAY, EVEN IN THE WINS.

4   Jill Siler, Twitter, April 15, 2019, https://twitter.com/jillmsiler/status/1117983220249825281?s=20.

Find the Good

Earlier this year we commemorated 9/11. This was the first time in my school career, eighteen years later, where not one class of students was even alive on September 11, 2001. Out of our entire student body, in fact, only nineteen students were born before that tragic event. As time passes, we have to work harder and harder to teach students about those events, much like my parents taught me about the assassination of John F. Kennedy and the days leading up to the Bay of Pigs, or like my grandparents taught me about World War II.

Our middle school did an exceptional job this past year with the 9/11 event. Each of the teachers wrote stories about where they were on that day and posted the stories on their classroom doors for students to see and read. They invited the high school band to their campus, and we all went outdoors to our flagpole, where our principal and one of our incredible social studies teachers shared words about the events that occurred on that day—both the horrific tragedy and the inspiring heroism of our first responders. The band began to play, and the flag was raised to half-mast. The social studies teacher reminded us that our flag stands for a country birthed from freedom, that our flag stands for the first responders who ran toward the danger and not away, that our flag stands for the land of the free and the home of the brave. And for the first time, in a long time, we *exclaimed* our pledge of allegiance.

The events of 9/11 were horrific, but the beauty of 9/12 was overwhelming. People coming out of their homes and out of their comfort zones to embrace one another, serve one another, and love one another. Freelance writer Elizabeth S. Gray wrote these words:

> I miss 9/12.
>
> I would never want another 9/11, but I miss the America of 9/12. Stores ran out of flags to sell because they were being flown everywhere.

People were Americans before they were upper/lower class, Jewish/Christian, Republican/Democrat. We hugged people without caring if they ate Chik-fil-A or wore Nikes.

On 9/12, what mattered more to us was what united us, not divided us.[5]

This was a horrific event, yet moments of kindness and good came from it. The same is true with all of our challenging moments. Even in the greatest grief, there are glimpses of goodness, kindness, and love. You still wish the event never happened, but you are thankful for those moments where you get to see the good in the world.

My encouragement to all of us is to find the good in those moments where you feel like there is none. Is the negative social media thread actually coalescing your school community in an unexpected and positive way? Have the ramifications of a poor choice by one of your students prompted a larger change in behavior by their classmates? Has the grievance that was filed actually made your organization better by shedding light on a real issue? Has the health diagnosis of someone within your organization given your community an opportunity to show love in a real and special way?

One of the things I love about my job is the opportunity to meet people from all over our state who are doing incredible things for kids every day. One of those people is Lawana Pulliam from Canadian ISD in Texas. She launched a podcast about personal leadership, and one thing she says at the end of every podcast is to "be the good."[6] Our charge is to be the good in the world. But our charge as leaders is to find the good, see the good, and share the good with others.

---

5   Elizabeth S. Gray, Imgur, September 11, 2018, https://k1025.com/i-miss-912 -united-we-used-to-stand/.

6   Lawana Pulliam, "Why in the World Am I Podcasting?" June 6, 2019, https:// lawana.home.blog/2019/05/06/why-in-the-world-am-i-podcasting/.

Conclusion

While this chapter is about how time helps challenging moments pass, Abraham Lincoln's statement is a reminder that the opposite is true as well. Incredible moments will pass away as well. But Lincoln doesn't stop there, and I hope we won't, either. Lincoln finishes the speech I referenced earlier with these words:

> And yet let us hope it is not quite true. Let us hope, rather, that by the best cultivation of the physical world, beneath and around us; and the intellectual and moral world within us, we shall secure an individual, social, and political prosperity and happiness, whose course shall be onward and upward, and which, while the earth endures, shall not pass away.[7]

Dr. Ervin Knezek, founder of lead4ward, an educational group that supports teachers and leaders, shared, "Yes, with the 5 percent, this too shall pass, but it is through that 5 percent that the 95 percent becomes richer, stronger, and more enduring."[8]

Our goal is to bask in the 95 percent of what we love, and understand that the 5 percent of challenging moments will happen. And we hope to thrive through those moments. But our ultimate goal would be to secure a personal, organizational, and cultural "prosperity and happiness" that would not pass, knowing that the 5 percent is what sometimes makes the 95 percent so rich and beautiful.

---

7   Abraham Lincoln's Speech to the Wisconsin State Agricultural Society (1859), http://www.abrahamlincolnonline.org/lincoln/speeches/fair.htm.

8   Ervin Knezek, founder of lead4ward, email to author, September 25, 2019, https://lead4ward.com/about/the-crew/.

5 TIPS TO THRIVE

1 Go do something for *you* this week: go see a movie, get a mani-pedi with a friend, go take a walk or bike ride outside.

2 The next time you have major feelings, instead of taking your mind off them, sit in them for a while. Get to the source of what's causing your hurt, and sift through those reasons.

3 Rock the "little things." Whether it is lunch duty or filling out the fourteenth spreadsheet of the day or picking up trash as you walk through campus, *be awesome* at it!

4 Find the good: be intentional as you go through your day, and find specific ways your colleagues or students are doing incredible things—and tell them!

5 *Be* the good: think about something you could do to make someone's day and then *do it*!

Nothing lasts forever - not even your troubles.
— Arnold H. Glasow

This Too Shall Pass

Thrive Through the Five by Jill M. Siler

Find Solace

Restore our hearts and minds to lead another day

New Month

Let Time Work for You

air out the situation

We have to be intentional with our most precious resources - ourselves and our time

Be Faithful in the Little Things

When we are faithful in our journey - even when we feel like our work is that of a mustard seed - success will follow.

things will get better

LONG-TERM GOAL

Find the Good

see the good

be the good

share the good

It is more than a mindset or an optimistic hope. It is the reality that whatever situation we are facing will get better. The speed at which it improves and the degree to which it improves are dependent on the situation itself.

Sketchnote by Amelia Buchanan
@edtech_amelia

FRAMEWORK TO THRIVE: TIME

Think back to the last thing that happened that really shook you or made you want to crawl under a rock . . .		
How long did you think it would take before you felt better about the situation?	How long did it actually take?	What actions did you take that helped you through that time?

What is an example of a "little thing" to which you were faithful that ended up benefiting you down the road?

What are some "little things" that you might look at differently moving forward?

How does the understanding that "this too shall pass" can be an asset help you think about thriving in the 5 percent?

FOURTEEN

MAKE A CHANGE

*Change is the law of life. And those
who look only to the past or present
are certain to miss the future.*

—JOHN F. KENNEDY

When I originally wrote the 2019 blog that inspired this book, I had the entire text ready to go for weeks, and I was just sitting on it, knowing that something was missing.

But I couldn't put my finger on it. . .

I'd written about how much I love what I do, but how there is this small percent of my work and of life that is really difficult. I'd shared my thoughts around how to lead through adversity and not just survive, but thrive. But something was missing. And I realized it was this. Sometimes . . .

Sometimes, perhaps the answer is to *make a change*.

I feel that each of us has been called into this great work with the purpose of making school an incredible place for students to learn and grow, but sometimes there are circumstances that prohibit you from achieving that purpose. Maybe it is a leader in the organization or the school community that is a roadblock, or maybe you just come to a place where you discern that your vision is no longer in alignment with the school community. Or perhaps another road calls to you.

Change is, literally, unsettling. And the decision is never easy and rarely clear. You may decide to stay and continue to serve all of the people (young and old) well, or you may decide to take the leap to serve elsewhere. Neither decision is right or wrong. My point is that this life is too short for us not to love what we do. The work is hard, no doubt. But when the ratio is tipping the other direction or the seasons or hard times extend to months and years, *be brave enough* to have an honest conversation with yourself about what change is needed, and *be bold enough* to start taking steps toward that end.

WHEN YOU NO LONGER LOVE WHAT YOU DO, BE BRAVE ENOUGH TO THINK ABOUT WHAT CHANGE IS NEEDED AND BE BOLD ENOUGH TO START TAKING STEPS TOWARD THAT END.

I have made several major changes and transitions in my life, and each has been a mixture of emotions: excitement, nervousness, sadness, fear, joy.

I've talked at length about my transition to the superintendency, but the transition to leadership in general was the first time that I decided to make a change. I absolutely loved teaching. I loved my colleagues and the camaraderie that we shared. I loved seeing the direct impact I had on kids and the privilege of watching these young adults grow, learn, and develop every single day.

But at the same time, I knew I had talents that would help me be successful at a different level. So I felt torn between a desire to stay in the classroom and the calling I felt to take that step forward. Watching a beloved coach on my campus transition to the role of assistant principal was what really showed me that *every* role can impact kids; each just looks a little different.

When I took my first assistant principal role I loved that, too, and loved the new community I was in. But not even twenty-four months after I got the job, my assistant superintendent decided to move to a new district and asked me to come with her. Again, I was faced with an unbelievable opportunity embedded in a ridiculously difficult decision—because I loved what I was doing yet was hopeful about what I could be doing.

Change is rarely easy. Excellence experts James Belasco and Ralph Stayer note, "Change is hard because people overestimate the value of what they have—and underestimate the value of what they may gain by giving that up."[1] I think for many of us that is true. There is so much good in our lives, and it's difficult to conceptualize "what could be." We know that the grass is not always greener on the other side, and so the last thing we want to do is put ourselves through a big transition for naught.

I've shared about my concerns as I made that last transition to the superintendency and the worries and fears I held around that. And that I still struggle with what my future might hold. No one wants to uproot their family or their lives unless it is absolutely going to be worth it. But it's hard to know the worth when you haven't lived that life yet.

WHEN CONSIDERING A CHANGE, IT IS HARD TO KNOW THE WORTH WHEN YOU HAVEN'T LIVED THAT LIFE YET.

---

1   James A. Belasco and Ralph C. Stayer, *Flight of the Buffalo: Soaring to Excellence, Learning to Let Employees Lead* (New York: Grand Central Publishing, 1994).

You'll notice, though, that I did not title this chapter "Time to Change Jobs," but rather "Make a Change." Because change can be different for different people in different contexts. Change might be altering your roles and responsibilities, or change might be assuming a new responsibility. Change might be something in the professional realm or something altogether personal that impacts our professional work, like starting a new exercise program or finding an outlet to relieve stress. A change might be finding a new mentor or mentoring someone yourself. Or it might be getting a coach. There are no limits to what change can look like or how it can benefit you.

So how do you know when it's time to make a change? And what kind of change could and should you make?

PRACTICAL TRUTHS TO POWERFULLY LEAD THROUGH MAKING A CHANGE

When the Scales Tip

I joked that I based this book on the 95-to-5 ratio but that there have been seasons where my percentage breakdown has been 85-to-15 or worse. And remember, the 5 percent is speaking to the truly difficult things—the things that keep you up at night. The counsel I would share on this is that your level of happiness and joy and the depths of your purpose have to be looked at from a thirty-thousand-foot view. The decision doesn't come after a difficult day, or a difficult week, or even a difficult semester. But we can and should make a change when those difficult seasons last longer, come more often, or never change.

The author and work-life expert Kathy Caprino asks the question this way when counseling people on whether to make a change:

> The majority of the time, are you feeling unhappy, depressed, thwarted, bored, misunderstood, mistreated? Do you feel that the "real you" just can't come out in this job, and the way you love to work isn't honored or respected?

Do you wonder how you ever ended up here, and fantasize daily about doing something very different?"[2]

The scales can tip when we are not being used for our greatest potential. Daniel Pink shares, "Human beings have an innate inner drive to be autonomous, self-determined, and connected to one another. And when that drive is liberated, people achieve more and live richer lives."[3] When we lose any one of those things (autonomy, mastery, or purpose) in our work or lives, the scales may begin to tip.

And probably my favorite thought on whether we need to make a change is from Seth Godin, who brilliantly describes the difference between a mere job and the opportunity to create value through our work:

> Your job is an historical artifact. It's a list of tasks, procedures, alliances, responsibilities, to-dos, meetings (mostly meetings) that were layered in, one at a time, day after day, for years.
>
> And your job is a great place to hide.
>
> Because, after all, if you're doing your job, how can you fail? Get in trouble? Make a giant error?
>
> The work, on the other hand, is the thing you do that creates value. This value you create, the thing you do like no one else can do, is the real reason we need you to be here, with us.
>
> When you discover that the job is in the way of the work, consider changing your job enough that you can go back to creating value.
>
> Anything less is hiding.[4]

---

2   Kathy Caprino, "5 Undeniable Signs It's Time to Leave Your Job," *Forbes*, February 14, 2017, https://www.forbes.com/sites/kathycaprino/2017/02/14/5-undeniable-signs-its-time-to-leave-your-job/#48f53e331539.

3   Daniel Pink, *Drive: The Surprising Truth About What Motivates Us* (New York: Riverhead Books, 2009).

4   Seth Godin, "So Busy Doing My Job I Can't Get Any Work Done," June 21, 2016, https://seths.blog/2016/06/so-busy-doing-my-job-i-cant-get-any-work-done/.

Sometimes we need to make a change professionally so that we can get back to creating value in what we do.

When You are Surrounded by Toxicity

Life is too short to put yourself in a toxic environment every day. You might try to improve the situation first. There are often several channels to share concerns with others in organizations. And your work in that, though not without risk, could pave a path for a healthier working community for the future. But sometimes that avenue is not fruitful. And that could warrant a change. Perhaps the change is to another campus; maybe it's to another school district or organization altogether. And I would hate for this to be the case for anyone, but perhaps out of education itself. The reality is that education means we will have to deal with a small number of people who say and do things that are hard to stomach. And dealing with that is part of the job. We have to understand that that's a part of it and find ways to love the big picture anyway.

When You're Ready!

Both of the reasons above are negative, but I would be remiss not to say that one of the biggest reasons to make a change is that you are ready! I have had the privilege to be a part of the design team for our state's Aspiring Superintendent Academy, and we gathered a focus group of aspiring superintendents and asked them for their feedback about the academy they participated in the year before and what we could do to make it even better for the next year. One suggestion this focus group gave was to find ways to help these aspiring leaders determine their readiness—such a poignant thought. So how do you know when you're ready?

I would love to say that you just know. But I'm going to be honest. I did not know if I was ready for the superintendency. (And by the way, I was.) But if you would've asked me, my answer would have been that I wasn't. And I think part of it is that maybe you're never ready until you just jump in and do it.

A big indicator of a time for change has always come from my mentors. When they encourage me to take the next step, then I give that some weight and reflect on what they're saying—and how I'm feeling about what they're saying.

Sometimes you need to make a change because you have accomplished everything you feel you can, and you're ready for the next challenge. I am a believer that you can always grow and improve and make something better. That's why I am still in my current district. But there is merit in saying, "I have been an assistant principal for five years and am fully competent in this role and ready for the next one."

I love talking with people who are at the next level above me and listening to their conversations. When I find that I am putting myself in their shoes and thinking what I would have done and realizing that it would have been a good solution or strategy, that is an indicator that I'm ready to make the change. One of my most vivid memories as a teacher was debriefing with my department chair after he had his department chair meeting with the campus principal. Since we shared the same conference period, he would often debrief with me after those meetings, asking how I would have handled different situations. Those sessions absolutely helped me realize that I needed to become a leader and was ready.

Making a change can happen because we have to or we need to or we want to. And any of those reasons can result in a great next best step.

Professional Change

When you know it is time for a change, you need to assess where you are and where you would like to be. Think about the people in your organization. Who do you want to emulate? What jobs would you love to hold? And what would you need to do in order to get there?

I am the first to say that you need to be mindful about your path; lateral moves can be challenging on a résumé. But sometimes when you're fleeing a toxic situation, that simply doesn't matter in the moment. Your great work will continue to build your reputation and résumé along the way. Also, sometimes a lateral move can give you a broader perspective or even be the first step to a greater opportunity down the road.

Make sure your yes is on the table and be open to a lot of different possibilities, even if the job doesn't look like the one you had envisioned or the organization doesn't seem like a perfect fit for you. Great things can come from unexpected places, so don't discount something before it even presents itself as an opportunity.

Personal Change

The average tenure of a superintendent in Texas is a little less than three years in a single district, and I just celebrated my eighth year. One of the ways I have continued to thrive is by continuing to grow and challenge myself. I was very open with my school board when I interviewed that I would love to continue to teach even in my role as superintendent. Several years ago, I had the great opportunity to join the University of North Texas as an adjunct professor. Connecting with students has reinvigorated my leadership skills in a very unexpected way.

GREAT THINGS CAN COME FROM UNEXPECTED PLACES, SO DON'T DISCOUNT SOMETHING BEFORE IT EVEN PRESENTS ITSELF AS AN OPPORTUNITY.

A few years into my superintendency, I became very concerned with becoming complacent. Our district was performing so well in many arenas, but I knew that we needed to continue to raise the bar. I accepted the invitation to join our state's Future-Ready Superintendent Leadership Network,[5] surrounding myself with a completely new peer group that pushed my thinking forward. And even this new venture in writing has been a personal change that has had massive professional impact on my work as a superintendent. I am more thoughtful. I process my stress differently. I am always looking for lessons in what I'm doing. And I am much more reflective in my decision-making.

Personal change can look absolutely different for everyone, yet it can have a significant impact on leaders. As author Joe Farcht writes, personal leadership is:

> the self-confident ability to crystallize your thinking and establish an exact direction for your own life, to commit yourself to moving in that direction, and then to take determined action to acquire, accomplish, or become whatever you identify as the ultimate goal for your life.[6]

Conclusion

Whether a change is good or bad, whether it was your choice or not, whether it is personal or professional, don't underestimate the impact that change can have. Change is hard, even when it is for the best reasons and even when you are loving the impact it is having. I look back at the job transitions I've made, and none occurred without tears. When you lead from your heart, you invest in the people around you, so when it comes time to transition, it is hard. In the same way, whenever you broach personal change, that is not without cost, either. But

---

5   The Future-Ready Superintendents Leadership Network (FRSLN) is a superintendent-designed and superintendent-led group of future-focused school leaders who gather for events that provide authentic learning experiences. Check it out here: www.futurereadytx.org/key-players/frsln/.

6   Joe Farcht, *Building Personal Leadership* (New York: Morgan James, 2007).

the benefits that can come when we are bold and make these changes can enrich our lives and impact those of the people we work with.

Even as I started this process of sharing my writing, it has been more of an internal roller coaster than a steady path toward growth or success. I asked my husband after publishing one of my first posts, "At what point will I not want to vomit when doing this?" I'm happy to report that after a few months of publicly sharing pieces on my blog, my desire to find a rock and crawl under it has transformed into mere subtle waves of nausea when I hit Publish. (Baby steps, friends . . . and don't even get me started about the roller coaster of writing this book!) But as in all things, when we're *bold* and do what we know we're being called to do, our work will impact others.

Be bold! Be brave! Put your yes on the table, consider what could be in your own life, and just take that next best step.

5 TIPS TO THRIVE

1 Think about your biggest issue right now and determine what kind of change needs to happen to make it better. Is it personal? Professional?

2 Put your yes on the table—even if it's just to look at it from all angles. Instead of allowing the default "no" to shut down the conversation, think about what the "yes" could be, and spend some time envisioning the possibilities.

3 Talk with a mentor and share your thoughts and possible next steps. Ask them what else you could or should be thinking about.

4 If you're struggling to pinpoint what is causing dissatisfaction, think back to Pink's autonomy, mastery, and purpose. Is there one aspect that could be better? Reflect on how that could be improved.

5 Know that change is and will be hard. Don't wait for it to get easy. Just start making small steps toward the change when you know it's the right thing to do.

Change is the law of life, and those who look only to the past or present are certain to miss the future. -John F. Kennedy

Make a Change
Thrive Through the Five by Jill M. Siler

When the Scales Tip

OPPORTUNITY

JOB

When You Are Surrounded by Toxicity

life is too short

When You're Ready

✓
✓
✓
○ You Are Ready!

jump in and do it!

Professional Change

Who are the people you want to emulate?

What jobs would you love to hold?

What would you need in order to get there?

be mindful about your path

Personal Change

be bold

be brave

There are no limits on what change can look like or how it can benefit you.

sketchnote by Amelia Buchanan
@edtech_amelia

FRAMEWORK TO THRIVE: MAKING A CHANGE

When was the last time you made a decision to change something major?	Describe the change. Was it personal or professional?	How did you know it was the right change to make?

As you look at your life right now, what changes do you see on the horizon?

What will indicate that it is time to make another change?

How does the understanding that sometimes it is time for a change help you think about thriving in the 5 percent?

CONCLUSION

The twelve most important inches in leadership
are those between your head and your heart.
Lead not just from a place of knowledge but
from a place of values and beliefs.

THE TWELVE MOST IMPORTANT INCHES IN LEADERSHIP

Wherever you go, go with all your heart.

—CONFUCIUS

The thing about the 5 percent is that most of the time you don't even know when it is coming. You are deep in the work, laser-focused on the most critical issues at hand (that seem critical at the time)—when something sweeps you into a completely different plane. And all of a sudden, your perspective is changed . . . sometimes forever.

I remember the morning of 9/11 well. It's the kind of date that needs no year attached. I was a teacher and a swim coach, and I had just finished morning practice. I had first-period athletics and had changed clothes and made my way to school. The entire campus was eerily quiet. The teacher next door was my "work mom," and she was always bringing in homemade goodies. She kept them in the same place, and my morning ritual was to walk into her first-period class and say a quick hello and sneak a special treat. I walked in that morning, and her class was intently watching something on the classroom TV. I didn't think twice about it—she taught AP US history, and they often viewed historical events and then deeply discussed their impact on history and their lives. She wasn't in the room at the time, and I think I even made a joke to her students not to tell her that I had stolen a piece of her homemade bread. They looked at me oddly, and I walked quietly to my room. I turned on the computer. My phone rang. And my worldview changed forever.

I wasn't a leader at that time, and I wonder now what they experienced that morning: what questions they faced, what uncertainties they tackled, what students and parents they had to calm. The only thing I know for certain is this: it was unprecedented.

Fast-forward nearly twenty years, and I think I'll remember spring break of 2020 just as well. Our district had an early March spring break, and the novel coronavirus, COVID-19, was just beginning to impact our country, though it was largely unseen in Texas. We had one patient who had been evacuated from the *Diamond Princess* cruise ship at a military base in San Antonio (six hours away) and one patient in Houston (five hours away) who had traveled to Egypt. On Friday, March 6, our last day of school before spring break, Austin canceled its South by Southwest festival (with only eight cases in Texas and none in the Austin area), giving up hundreds of millions in revenue. We all realized then that this was a big deal.

What was planned as a family vacation week quickly turned into crisis planning as the virus began to spread across the nation and our state. The first decision was whether we should close. I had been through this before. I understood the weight of these decisions. But who closes an entire district without a single confirmed case in your community or county? But we were sending thousands of students and families all across the world for spring break to places that had been impacted by the virus, and they were about to return to us.

Our state's commissioner of education provided tremendous leadership and began to hold daily calls with superintendents throughout the crisis. His team shared what we needed to do if we closed and some health strategies in case we decided to open. We were all considering closing—if only for a week to give us more time to make a more informed decision. But in the midst of one of those early calls, he said, "If we close [after spring break], be prepared for the possibility that you won't reopen." Those words were critical in helping me understand that this was no longer just a decision about closure; this was a decision about how we were going to completely overhaul education for the long haul—in a matter of days. Absolutely unprecedented.

In times of crisis, it all comes down to the *how*. How will you lead in a way that inspires hope that you *can* and *will* thrive through this season? How do you lead with both your *head* and your *heart*?

IT'S NOT SO MUCH THE WHAT. ANYONE CAN KNOW WHAT TO DO. IT'S ALL ABOUT THE HOW. HOW WILL YOU LEAD IN A WAY THAT INSPIRES HOPE?

Here is what that first week looked like for us.

Monday's Mission: Contact Every Kid

We knew we had to collect critical information about technology needs (devices and internet), *and* we wanted to let our students know that they were cared for and *missed*!

> **Head:** Assigned every teacher a group of students and created a script to collect specific information. Created a central document for all of the information.

> **Heart:** Underscored the main purpose was to *connect* with kids and find out their family's needs. Shared stories and pictures of our staff connecting with their students. We connected with nearly every student in a matter of days.

Tuesday's Task: Tune Up Your Tech

Transitioning to online learning requires a *lot* of learning, and we wanted to be thoughtful about what that transition would look like. This activity allowed our teachers to start with the end in mind and gain some tech tools along the way.

Head: Shared one of the coolest online schools we could find and had teachers walk through a lesson. Had them read an article of fifteen tips for online learning. Asked them to download a video conferencing tool. Had them learn the basics of hyperdocs. Asked them to complete a reflection form on their learning.

Heart: Chose lessons in that online school that showed teachers connecting with kids in unique ways. Chose an article that really focused on the social-emotional aspect of online learning (core tenets of *less is more, capture kids' hearts, video and human connection is important*). Asked them to videoconference their team in order to connect with them. Created a mini-online hyperdocs lesson, connecting them to their purpose. Structured the online reflection to evoke emotion and infuse content.

Wednesday's Workshop: Work on Week 1

From the data we collected Monday, we realized we had to start low-tech and transition slowly to high-tech.

Head: Laid out the two phases in our transition to remote learning. We'd start with low-tech learning activities that could be done at home with books and resources we sent home. We'd then transition to high-tech activities once we equipped students with devices and internet access, using online learning platforms. Created step-by-step instructions on how to prepare work for week 1.

Heart: Started the day's assignment with a video recap of what we had done that week (pictures from social media, pictures of the learning that happened on Tuesday) and then walked through what we were about to do and why we were doing it.

Thursday's Thoughtfulness

The activity from Wednesday needed two days to complete, but we wanted to check in on our staff socially and emotionally.

Head: Included a video that was part of a series that our high school students had been watching as part of their "Tiger Talks" time (a thirty-minute family meeting time of 12–15 students with one staff member facilitating). Included a list of intentional, quick actions to help foster a sense of gratitude for the incredible work that was happening all around them.

Heart: The video was moving. It not only reminded us that students would be struggling during this time, it was a profound call to action to prevent the virus from spreading and to remain rooted in love throughout. The assignment included links to some of the great (and funny) things our staff had been a part of. For instance, our softball coach assigned a daily challenge, like record a workout session, and we published funny video compilations of the highlights. Our band directors also created daily music videos of them playing (six feet apart) various songs they thought their students would love. And it closed with a reminder that I loved them.

Friday: Family Day

The bulk of the work was done. Materials distribution had been set up, and a thousand students were about to arrive on our campuses to pick up books, learning materials, locker contents, and devices, Chick-fil-A style. Staff volunteered to do curbside delivery, but outside of their shift, we encouraged them to rest and get mentally prepared for the week to come!

> **Head:** Outlined the curbside pickup process.

> **Heart:** The only assignment for the day was for our staff to spend some extra time with their families. Leading with heart means recognizing that while a typical workweek is 8–4, M–F, sometimes our educators have to work around the clock, and there is no need to work for the sake of work.[1]

It was full speed ahead from the start of the pandemic: communicating, planning, serving, creating, listening—everything that comes with being a leader. It was head-down kind of work. But one morning, late in that first week, I stepped onto our campuses and *saw* the work (the amazing, incredible, significant *work*) that our people had been doing, and the tears began to flow.

There was no other place we would all rather be than *in* school on that Thursday morning. And what we were asking of *everyone* (teachers, parents, students) was unfathomable. But here they were, *rising up* and doing all that we had asked and so much more!

It was a pinnacle moment that brought such clarity to my profound thankfulness for all of our teachers and staff—and to all of the teachers across our nation, who were doing the very same thing! That week, South Carolina School Board member Ken Buck shared this post to Facebook, which was in turn shared by many:

> We gave educators almost no notice. We asked them to completely redesign what school looks like and in about 24 hours local administrators and teachers "Apollo 13'ed"

---

1   To see all of the steps that Gunter ISD took to lead through the coronavirus crisis, visit: jillmsiler.com/covid-19/.

the problem and fixed it. Kids learning, children being fed, needs being met in the midst of a global crisis.

No state agency did this, no so-called national experts on curriculum. The local educators fixed it in hours. HOURS.

In fact, existing state and federal policies actually created multiple roadblocks. Local schools figured out how to do it around those, too. No complaining and no hand-wringing—just solutions and amazingly clever plans.

Remember that the next time someone tries to convince you that schools are better run by mandates from non-educators. Remember that the next time someone tells you that teachers have it easy or try to persuade you that educators are not among the smartest, most ingenious people in society. And please never say to me again, "Those who can't do anything else just go into teaching."

Get out of the way of a teacher and watch with amazement at what really happens.[2]

Throughout that first long and trying week, there were so many sources of encouragement—including my own staff and community members, and leaders I knew and some I didn't from across the state. One fellow leader reached out and shared, "Some leaders are great at taking care of people. Some are great at taking care of tasks. Very few are able to take care of both at such a high level. YOU are one of those leaders." Really kind words, but clearly this underlines the impact of the twelve inches between the head (the *what*: the tasks) and the heart (the *how*: the people).

---

2   Ken Buck, Facebook, March 18, 2020, https://www.facebook.com/kenbuck/posts/10158290606057249.

PRACTICAL TRUTHS TO POWERFULLY LEAD FROM THE HEART

It Starts from the Top

This past fall my leadership team read *The Culture Code* by Daniel Coyle, in which the author shares fascinating stories about highly successful teams, from the Navy's SEAL Team Six to a group of master jewel thieves. One of his stories is about the San Antonio Spurs. He paints a picture of how head coach Gregg Popovich builds culture in his team through individual connection, sharing truths about performance, and letting athletes see the greater impact of their lives in this world. He shares one story about the 2013 NBA Championship Series, where the Spurs were up three games to two over Miami and were so poised to win that they booked a special celebratory dinner at a local restaurant. They in fact did not win—but Pop ushered the team to the restaurant anyway, rearranging the tables so they were closer together. Coyle shares:

> Popovich stood and greeted every player as they came through the door. Some got a hug, some got a smile, some got a joke or a light touch on the arm. The wine flowed. They sat and ate together. Popovich moved around the room, connecting with each player in turn. People later said he behaved like the father of a bride at a wedding, taking time with everyone, thanking them, appreciating them. There were no speeches, just a series of intimate conversations. In a moment that could have been filled with frustration, recrimination, and anger, he filled their cup.[3]

There are many things that my incredible team is responsible for and has made happen. But when it comes to culture and how we lead,

---

3   Daniel Coyle, *The Culture Code: The Secrets of Highly Successful Groups* (New York: Bantam, 2018).

it starts with me. As leaders, we are faced with situations daily, and how we lead matters! When we're going through a really difficult time, we still have control over how we react and how we lead. And like Pop, even in the worst of times we can still behave like a parent of the bride and celebrate the greater things in life.

Love Is Action

Sometimes I work with incredible leaders who are struggling with morale or building a culture, and there is a disconnect. When I talk with these leaders, they share an unending love and appreciation for their teams, but when I hear from their followers, they don't feel it. That's the funny thing about love. It can exist in concept, but unless it's outwardly shared with others, it is only known by the owner.

If you've never heard of Bob Goff, you must check him out: he has a larger-than-life love for others and is renowned for his relationship with sweet Maria Goff. One of his best-selling books is *Love Does*,[4] and the opening describes that while many of us have big dreams, we don't always do the things necessary to achieve them. He writes:

> It becomes clear that we need to stop plotting the course and instead just land the plane on our plans to make a difference by getting to the "do" part of our faith. That's because love is never stationary. In the end, love doesn't just keep thinking about it or keep planning for it. Simply put: love does.

This then begs the question: How do we "do" love with the people we work with and lead? Author Mark Nation sums it up in four simple steps (and a clever acronym): listening, openness, vulnerability, and empathy.[5] He says, "*Love*. It's the chief activator that makes

---

4 Bob Goff, *Love Does: Discover a Secretly Incredible Life in an Ordinary World* (Nashville: Thomas Nelson, 2012).

5 Mark Nation, "Leadership is a Four-Letter Word," *Forbes*, July 1, 2019, https://www.forbes.com/sites/forbescoachescouncil/2019/07/01/leadership-is-a-four-letter-word/#5d71ea4a5d45.

the greatest performances, and greatest people, possible. At its very heart, leadership is love." As we begin to really listen (and not just silently prepare your next contribution to the conversation, as I am often guilty of doing), be open with one another, be vulnerable, and show empathy to those you work with, we start to "do" love. Amber Teamann and Melinda Miller show this in practice in *Lead with Appreciation*. Amber writes:

> If a teacher posts about being up all night with a crying, sick baby, I want to meet that teacher at the door with grace and a latte. If I know a teacher is heading off for a family reunion because Grandma is in poor health, I want to ask about Grandma when that teacher returns. It's these little things that can make a world of difference to a teacher.[6]

Last summer, I had the privilege of meeting the writer and speaker Todd Gongwer. After a career in business and athletics and as someone who works with organizational culture, he set out to write a book about all of the impactful ideas he had seen along his professional path. He drafted a table of contents with all of the points he wanted to drive home, but what came out in the end was a beautiful parable about a janitor who taught a coach (and a community) how to lead. In his closing, he writes, "Leadership is all about your influence. And when you as leaders truly decide to lead from the heart with a genuine desire to fulfill your purpose, you immediately jump on the path to being the type of leader you were called to be."[7]

It's Not About You

We are fortunate in our district to have incredible school board members, but as a newly minted superintendent, I went from having one

---

6   Melinda Miller and Amber Teamann, *Lead with Appreciation: Fostering a Culture of Appreciation* (San Diego, Dave Burgess Consulting, Inc., 2019).

7   Todd Gongwer, *Lead . . . for God's Sake: A Parable for Finding the Heart of Leadership* (Carol Stream, IL: Tyndale, 2010).

boss to having seven. As a superintendent, you go from having supervisors who have had the same kind of background, education, and experiences as you to working for seven people with varying backgrounds. I quickly learned that the better you are at working with your board and building a cohesive "team of eight," the more successful your district can become. But what did that look like? I struggled at first. At one point early in my superintendency, I went out to visit now-retired superintendent Dr. Jerome Stewart (who was serving as superintendent at Midlothian ISD), and I'll never forget what he shared with me: "Jill, my role as a superintendent with my board is to be a shepherd. Find out how to love and serve them, and you will no longer struggle." In other words, Jill, it's not about you.

LEADERSHIP IS NOT ABOUT YOU. IT'S ABOUT HOW TO BEST LOVE AND SUPPORT THOSE YOU SERVE.

John Maxwell says it like this:

> Inexperienced leaders are quick to lead before knowing anything about the people they intend to lead. But mature leaders listen, learn, and then lead. They listen to their people's stories. They find out about their hopes and dreams. They become acquainted with their aspirations. And they pay attention to their emotions. From those things, they learn about their people. They discover what is valuable to them. And then they lead based upon what they've learned.[8]

---

8   John Maxwell, *The 21 Irrefutable Laws of Leadership: Follow Them and People Will Follow You* (Nashville: Thomas Nelson, 1998).

Leading is often more about serving from behind than leading in front. When we begin to truly understand and meet the needs of our people, we will know what it means to lead with our hearts.

Lead from the Heart

As we went through that financial crisis my first year of the superintendency, we ultimately lost 20 percent of our total staff. Most of them were voluntary departures through an early notice of resignation incentive program. But then we had to make the truly difficult decision to reduce the staff further through a "reduction in force" process. One of the lessons my dad, who served as a corporate CEO, taught me was to avoid "death by a thousand cuts." In other words, make the difficult decisions you have to and do it right . . . one time. We followed our policies. We communicated well and were transparent. We did it in the fairest way possible, knowing that it was absolutely necessary to save us from facing bankruptcy. We did it in the best way possible to be able to immediately start on the road to healing and recovery. And yet it was still horrific. The facts of the situation and the effective way that it was led didn't change the emotions. I cried. And not just by myself in private, but with our people. We grieved together.

But at the same time, I was comforted by knowing that even though what we were going through was terrible, there was no one else I would rather have sitting in that chair and making those decisions for this community than me. The great Maya Angelou said, "I've learned that people will forget what you said, people will forget what you did, but people will never forget how you made them feel." I learned how to lead with love and saw a community respond in love— and that was enough to sustain me (and us) through the most difficult of times.

In terms of the superintendency, none led with heart as well as Rocky Kirk. Dr. Kirk was a longtime leader in a district where I served. He had this innate ability to tap into your core purpose and make you *know* that you were valued, that this work was important, and that *you* were making the difference. But those of us who knew him well and had the privilege of hearing him speak knew that more often than not he would show powerful emotion when he spoke to others—because he cared so deeply about the impact we were having on kids. I don't think you ever fully appreciate that until you work under a leader who does not lead from a place of love. And I have never been prouder of my own leadership than in those moments where I, too, felt so passionately about what I was communicating and cared so deeply for those I was serving that I showed emotion like he did.

Conclusion

As I think about my future legacy in leadership, these words penned by Joelle Jay guide me:

> When you have achieved what you want to achieve . . .
> when you have become who you want to be . . .
> when you have done what you want to do . . .
> what will be true for you?[9]

What keeps playing in my mind as we come to the close of this book is that *we get to decide how to do this*. Leadership is not a scientific, step-by-step act that can be guided by an instructional manual. It is an art that ebbs and flows, where we must show strength and stability in one moment and compassion and grace in the next. But we can't give our kids our best until we are all in—and not just with our commitment, not just with our heads, but with our whole hearts.

As educators, we have the most incredible job in the world—to literally change lives through education. As leaders, we have a tremendous opportunity to shape the culture of an organization, to set the vision for where we want to go in our work and to be models of positive leadership. And as leaders, we decide how to do this—in a way that reaches people's hearts, in a way that touches and changes lives.

---

9   Joelle Jay, *The Inner Edge: The 10 Practices of Personal Leadership* (Santa Barbara, Praeger, 2009).

WE GET TO DECIDE HOW TO DO THIS. LEADERSHIP IS NOT A SCIENTIFIC ACT. IT IS AN ART THAT EBBS AND FLOWS, WHERE LEADERS CAN LEAD WITH STRENGTH AND STABILITY IN ONE MOMENT AND COMPASSION AND GRACE IN THE NEXT.

The 5 percent is part of it. We get to do *amazing* things for kids and teachers and our school communities, but **it is not without cost**. I have led through some of the most difficult challenges and seasons one can experience as a leader; many I have written about in this book, and many more I have not. They are not events I merely survived; they are the very events that have defined my leadership. They are milestones and memorials that demonstrate we can all thrive through the toughest moments of our journey. Be bold and lead with love!

THE 5 PERCENT DEFINES OUR LEADERSHIP. THE MILESTONES AND MEMORIALS OF THOSE EVENTS REMIND US THAT WE CAN LEAD WELL THROUGH THE TOUGHEST MOMENTS OF OUR JOURNEY. AND THE LEARNING AT EACH JUNCTURE BETTER INSTRUCTS US HOW TO TRULY THRIVE THROUGH THE FIVE.

5 TIPS TO THRIVE

1 Carve out thirty minutes a day to connect with the people in your organization. Stop at a campus as kids are walking in and pop in to every room just to say, "Happy Monday." Make a special point of asking about loved ones, and make a personal connection.

2 Put *love* into action this week through the acronym we learned: listen, be open, be vulnerable, and show empathy. Be intentional in your conversations to actively show that you care.

3 Go about your day remembering that it's not about you. Think about how you can serve the people around you, in big ways and small, and do it.

4 Remember that you can hold people to a really high standard and make really difficult decisions and still show love. The next time you have to walk someone through a mistake, remember that it can be done in love and with dignity.

5 As you lead this week, move your leadership twelve inches. Understand *what* you want to accomplish with your mind, but then bring it down to *how* you will do it with your heart.

FRAMEWORK TO THRIVE: LEAD FROM THE HEART

Who is a leader in your life who leads from the heart?

How is their impact different than other leaders you know?

What in this chapter has made you rethink your comfort and use of emotion in leadership?

How does the understanding that we must lead from our hearts help you think about thriving in the 5 percent?

THRIVE THROUGH THE FIVE

PRACTICAL TRUTHS TO POWERFULLY LEAD THROUGH CHALLENGING TIMES

written by
DR JILL M. SILER

sketchnote by Amelia Buchanan
@edtech_amelia

ACKNOWLEDGMENTS

It is absolutely surreal to write these words of acknowledgement for a book I didn't even know I would write just eighteen months ago. There are so many people who have helped along this journey.

It has to begin with Dave and Shelley Burgess. Dave—much like you did for teaching, and Shelley, much like you did for leading, you both have shattered the archetype for publishing by leveraging technology and social media to make what used to be out of reach for so many a real possibility . . . And that is giving amazing practitioners, who are doing the work every single day—who are not perfect but absolutely passionate—the chance to share their authentic voice with others. The vision for your work is crystal clear, as is the voice of each of your authors' manifestos. Thank you for saying yes to me and for supporting and encouraging me every step of the way. I am forever grateful for your trust.

To the entire team at the Reading List—you all have been *amazing* and have made this book better in every way! Lindsey and Sal—thank you for your leadership and knowing when to push but also for giving so much freedom in the process. Dana—thank you for digging deeply into the first draft. Your insights and edits were coveted, but your encouragement to me as a writer won't ever be forgotten! Liz—the interior design is absolutely beautiful! I didn't think I could love this book any more, until I opened it up and saw how you weaved every element of the story on our cover onto every page.

To Amelia Buchanan, what started as an admiration of your work on Twitter flourished into one of the most beautiful pieces of this book. Thank you for bringing every chapter to life and intricately weaving the deep message with a flair of whimsy. I love the stories you tell and the symbolism you use, and I cannot wait for the world to see your work in this way. (BTW, you can find Amelia on Twitter at @edtech_amelia and check out her work at aapruett.wixsite.com/jmuedtech.)

To Laci Bracewell, I'm not even sure where to start my thanks. You have coached me in more ways than I can count along this entire journey. Thanks for the crash course in marketing and business development and for teaching me the importance of personal brand. Thanks most of all for designing the brilliant cover that tells the powerful story that leadership (and life) is a journey and that we can and will thrive! (To see more of Laci's amazing designs, visit rubysrubbish.com.)

To Rebecca Egger, who pored over every single page and wrote incredible insights, helpful changes, and encouraging words that helped sustain me through this process—THANK YOU! Your fingerprints and poignant thoughts are on every page of this book. I will forever keep your edits and am so thankful I chose you to do the first read for me.

All dreams start somewhere, and I'm so thankful that the person to whom I first uttered the words "I want to write a book" was Amy Jacobs. You are an incredible leader, and I am so thankful we have been able to walk this journey together for twenty years. Thank you for being my confidant for pretty much every 5 percent season of my life and, most of all, for giving me the courage to do the very thing that had been laid on my heart!

To Lisa Harden, you've helped me walk this leadership journey since it began. Your friendship and your willingness to listen have been a gift, and your endless belief in me has helped me to continue to take bold steps. Thanks for always being just a phone call away!

To the people who helped me launch this book off the ground: Anna LeBaron, who gave me great counsel on the launch process and taught me the importance of building my platform in order to broaden my impact. And to Tara Martin, whose energy in launching every DBC book knows no bounds! Thank you both!

A HUGE thank-you to every author who answered my calls and emails and to those who continue to provide support and encouragement along this journey: Dr. Sandra Harris (*The Trust Factor* and others), Dr. Ervin Knezek (*Be Bold*), Tamara Letter (*A Passion for Kindness*), Tara Martin (*Be Real* and others), Melanie Mayer (*10 Miles to Go* and others), Thomas C. Murray (*Personal and Authentic* and others), Evan A. Robb (*The 10 Minute Principal* and others), Dr. Joe Sanfelippo (*Hacking Leadership* and others), and Amber Teamann (*Lead with Appreciation*).

I have been so blessed to have an amazing professional learning network—from my friends and colleagues on social media, to the incredible leaders at organizations like TASA, TCWSE, Region 10, AASA, TACS, and others. But I am so incredibly thankful for the #sistersupts I serve with in Texas and across this country . . . you all inspire me EVERY day! My goal is to be half the leader you all are!

To all the leaders who have led me . . . I can't even put into words how thankful I am for the impact you've had on my life. Thank you for showing me what it means to be a leader: Joe Kieke, Jamie Smith, David Manning, Alex Torrez, Dana Marable, Ernest Seitz, Ervin Knezek, Cynthia Clinesmith, Lisa Lawrence, Diane Frost, Becky Burnett, Susan Bohn, Myra Pettit, Rocky Kirk, and Jenny Preston.

To all of my Gunter ISD board members: Jeff Banks, Ron Box, L. D. Byrd, Dr. Gary Harris, Gabe Johnson, John Jonas, Candy Leonard, Dr. Kelly Martin, Scott Meyerdirk, Lynn Reed, and Steve Smith. You all have made me a better leader; you have taught me what excellence looks like in the superintendency. Thank you for supporting me in every season—but especially during the 5 percent.

To the teachers, staff, leadership team, and community of Gunter ISD: I am beyond blessed to be your superintendent. The stories I've written about in this book weren't stories for all of us . . . We lived through these trials and challenges together—and there's no one I'd rather lead with and for than all of you. I love you with all my heart.

To my mom and dad: For over fifty years, I've watched you walk through every season in life. Thank you for teaching me how to thrive in even the most trying times. Dad, I will always covet our talks around leadership. Thank you for teaching me how to boldly lead through the hardest issues. Mom, thank you for being the best mom a kid could ever have and for showing me that the people are always more important than the tasks! I'm so thankful for the impact you both have had on my life!

To William: Twenty years ago, you married a rookie teacher and coach without an inkling of what was to come. I could never have done nor do what I do without your support. Thanks for always believing in me! Thank you for always loving your family more than anything in the world and for always standing in the gap when I'm called to lead.

To Caitlyn and Caleb: There aren't words to describe the depths of my love for you both! Thank you for allowing me to write this book and lead the way that I do. My greatest hope is that you know more than anything else in the world that you are LOVED! May this book give you the courage to go after your greatest hopes and dreams—no matter how big or bold they are!

And last but not least, to every leader . . .

who has ever made the difficult decision;

who stands in the gap for the people they serve;

who truly understands how excruciating the 5 percent can be;

and who chooses to LEAD ANYWAY . . .

This book is for you!

ABOUT THE AUTHOR

DR. JILL SILER has been serving as the Superintendent of Gunter ISD, a growing school district an hour north of Dallas, since 2012. Jill grew up in Rochester and Buffalo, New York, and completed her undergraduate work at the University of Pittsburgh, where she was a collegiate swimmer. She moved to Austin in 1996 and began serving as a high school world geography teacher and swim coach at John B. Connally High School in Pflugerville ISD. Jill earned her master's from Texas State University and began her administrative career in Marble Falls ISD, where she served as the Assistant Principal for Instruction. In 2004, Jill went to Lake Travis ISD, where she served as a campus and district leader for eight years. During that time, she completed her doctorate at the University of Texas.

In her first months as a superintendent, Jill faced financial crisis along with many other challenges that leadership brings. In 2015, her school board was named a TASA Honor Board as one of the top 5 school boards in the state, and one of her campuses was named a 2017 National Blue Ribbon School. Jill is the Chair of the Future-Ready Superintendent Leadership Network (FRSLN) Design Team through the Texas Association of School Administrators (TASA), where innovative leaders from across the state gather to learn, share, and grow together.

Jill has a passion for helping others reach their goals and is the leader of TASA's Aspiring Superintendent Academy. She is a frequent speaker at Texas's First-Time Superintendent Academy as well as other leadership and education conferences. Her writing can be found on her website, jillmsiler.com. The blog that formed the foundation of this book was featured in the November 2019 edition of AASA's *School Administrator*, the national school leadership organization's publication.

Jill and her husband, William, have been married for twenty years and have two children: Caitlyn, who is fifteen years old and in tenth grade, and Caleb, who is eleven years old and in sixth grade.

BRING JILL M. SILER TO YOUR ORGANIZATION

JILL IS A PASSIONATE SPEAKER who inspires others to live and lead through engaging keynotes, workshops, and customized professional learning experiences. Dr. Siler's experience at every level (student, teacher, campus and district leader, and superintendent) gives her a unique perspective of the entire organization and an authentic voice that relates to all audiences. Through personal stories, Jill shares a powerful message that motivates people to take their next best step and thrive in any situation.

POPULAR MESSAGES FROM JILL M. SILER:

- Thrive through the Five: Inspiring Hope in Challenging Times
- The Unlikely Places from which Success Is Born: Leading through Failure, Fear, and Faith
- The 12 Most Important Inches in Leadership: Leading with Heart
- The 12 Most Important Inches in Teaching: Teaching with Heart
- Visioning What Could Be
- The Journey to Future-Ready
- Engaging around Contentious Issues
- You Are Enough: Balance, Self-Care, Mentorship
- Aspiring Leaders: Getting the Job and Being Successful in the Job
- The Most Important Thing: The Power of Our Teachers

For more information, visit jillmsiler.com, contact Jill at jillmsiler@gmail.com, or follow @jillmsiler on social media.

WHAT PEOPLE ARE SAYING ABOUT JILL M. SILER:

- Dr. Jill Siler pours herself into the future of education in the state of Texas through authentic relationship. This girl breathes LIFE into leaders. Find yourself a @jillmsiler. #TASA19 #Inspiring Leaders—@ccross22 (Candice Cross, principal, Lubbock-Cooper ISD)

- If you ever have the opportunity to learn from @jillmsiler, take it. Her sessions were relevant and timely. She always sends you away with things that will make you a better educator and leader. #R10Innovate—@mrthamilton (Trent Hamilton, assistant principal, Anna ISD)

- Great learning the last four days at #TASA20. @jillmsiler you are AMAZING—all the prep and passion you've put into everything that I've seen and been a part of has been such a blessing to receive! #AspiringSupts—@skimbriel (Stacy Kimbriel, principal, Plano ISD)

- Jill Siler teaches me how to be better EVERY SINGLE TIME I hear her speak!—@megantimme (Megan Timme, Region 10 director)

- Loved this quote, "Sometimes places like failure, fear, and faith are the very places from which greatness, hope, and success are born." Thanks for sharing, @jillmsiler! @R4TCWSE #Refined2019—@drgoffney (LaTonya Goffney, superintendent, Aldine ISD)

- Absolutely loved the enthusiasm from superintendent @jillmsiler from @Gunter_ISD regarding

- #DigitalTransformation. #TASA19—@lance_johanson (Lance Johanson, regional partner manager, ASCD)

"Our mission sometimes walks us through the valley of the shadow of doubt." So true, Jill Siler! Great keynote msg at #TCWSE2020 Conference.—@smilder (Scott Milder, founder of Friends of Texas Public Schools)

Just heard the amazing @jillmsiler! Wow! Wow! Wow! So inspiring! Oh, to be half the leader, motivator, speaker you are . . .—@atagle10 (Adriana Tagle, principal, Banquete ISD)

Keynote by @jillmsiler. Life-changing. #TCWSE2020— @paulapatterson (Paula Patterson, chief academic officer, Sheldon ISD)

Thank you, @jillmsiler, for your inspirational message today at @tasanet #FRSLN. I am inspired and excited to impact the next generation!—@duanabrashear (Duana Brashear, principal, Splendora ISD)

At what has been an amazing conference, these encouraging words: "When we are bold . . . when we choose action in the midst of fear . . . when we lead anyway . . . that courage is the birth of greatness." Thank you, @jillmsiler, for an incredibly moving message. #TCWSE2020—@kerrygain (Kerry Gain, chief academic officer, Del Valle ISD)

Inspired, listening to @jillmsiler facilitate discussion about the importance of driving positive culture in order to accomplish more. #R10Innovate—@jenandjelic (Jen Andjelic, principal, New Caney ISD)

Jill ALWAYS delivers!—@deannlee85 (Deann Lee, superintendent, Millsap ISD)

MORE FROM DAVE BURGESS Consulting, Inc.

Since 2012, DBCI has been publishing books that inspire and equip educators to be their best. For more information on our titles or to purchase bulk orders for your school, district, or book study, visit **DaveBurgessconsulting.com/DBCIbooks**.

MORE INSPIRATION, PROFESSIONAL GROWTH & PERSONAL DEVELOPMENT

Be REAL by Tara Martin

Be the One for Kids by Ryan Sheehy

The Coach ADVenture by Amy Illingworth

Creatively Productive by Lisa Johnson

Educational Eye Exam by Alicia Ray

The EduNinja Mindset by Jennifer Burdis

Empower Our Girls by Lynmara Colón and Adam Welcome

Finding Lifelines by Andrew Grieve and Andrew Sharos

The Four O'Clock Faculty by Rich Czyz

How Much Water Do We Have? by Pete and Kris Nunweiler

If the Dance Floor is Empty, Change the Song by Dr. Joe Clark

P Is for Pirate by Dave and Shelley Burgess

A Passion for Kindness by Tamara Letter

The Path to Serendipity by Allyson Apsey

Sanctuaries by Dan Tricarico

The SECRET SAUCE by Rich Czyz

Shattering the Perfect Teacher Myth by Aaron Hogan

Stories from Webb by Todd Nesloney

Talk to Me by Kim Bearden

Teach Better by Chad Ostrowski, Tiffany Ott, Rae Hughart, and
　　Jeff Gargas

Teach Me, Teacher by Jacob Chastain

Teach, Play, Learn! by Adam Peterson

TeamMakers by Laura Robb and Evan Robb

Through the Lens of Serendipity by Allyson Apsey

The Zen Teacher by Dan Tricarico

LIKE A PIRATE™ SERIES

Teach Like a PIRATE by Dave Burgess

eXPlore Like a Pirate by Michael Matera

Learn Like a Pirate by Paul Solarz

Play Like a Pirate by Quinn Rollins

Run Like a Pirate by Adam Welcome

Tech Like a PIRATE by Matt Miller

LEAD LIKE A PIRATE™ SERIES

Lead Like a PIRATE by Shelley Burgess and Beth Houf

Balance Like a Pirate by Jessica Cabeen, Jessica Johnson, and
　　Sarah Johnson

Lead beyond Your Title by Nili Bartley

Lead with Appreciation by Amber Teamann and Melinda Miller

Lead with Culture by Jay Billy

Lead with Instructional Rounds by Vicki Wilson

Lead with Literacy by Mandy Ellis

LEADERSHIP & SCHOOL CULTURE

Culturize by Jimmy Casas

Escaping the School Leader's Dunk Tank by Rebecca Coda and
　　Rick Jetter

From Teacher to Leader by Starr Sackstein

The Innovator's Mindset by George Couros

It's OK to Say "They" by Christy Whittlesey

Kids Deserve It! by Todd Nesloney and Adam Welcome

Live Your Excellence by Jimmy Casas

Let Them Speak by Rebecca Coda and Rick Jetter

The Limitless School by Abe Hege and Adam Dovico

Next-Level Teaching by Jonathan Alsheimer

The Pepper Effect by Sean Gaillard

The Principled Principal by Jeffrey Zoul and Anthony McConnell

Relentless by Hamish Brewer

The Secret Solution by Todd Whitaker, Sam Miller, and
      Ryan Donlan

Start. Right. Now. by Todd Whitaker, Jeffrey Zoul, and Jimmy Casas

Stop. Right. Now. by Jimmy Casas and Jeffrey Zoul

Teach Your Class Off by CJ Reynolds

They Call Me "Mr. De" by Frank DeAngelis

Unmapped Potential by Julie Hasson and Missy Lennard

Word Shift by Joy Kirr

Your School Rocks by Ryan McLane and Eric Lowe

TECHNOLOGY & TOOLS

50 Things You Can Do with Google Classroom by Alice Keeler
      and Libbi Miller

50 Things to Go Further with Google Classroom by Alice Keeler
      and Libbi Miller

140 Twitter Tips for Educators by Brad Currie, Billy Krakower,
      and Scott Rocco

Block Breaker by Brian Aspinall

Code Breaker by Brian Aspinall

Control Alt Achieve by Eric Curts

Google Apps for Littles by Christine Pinto and Alice Keeler

Master the Media by Julie Smith

Reality Bytes by Christine Lion-Bailey, Jesse Lubinsky, and
      Micah Shippee, PhD

Sail the 7 Cs with Microsoft Education by Becky Keene
      and Kathi Kersznowski

Shake Up Learning by Kasey Bell

Social LEADia by Jennifer Casa-Todd

Stepping up to Google Classroom by Alice Keeler and
    Kimberly Mattina

Teaching Math with Google Apps by Alice Keeler and
    Diana Herrington

Teachingland by Amanda Fox and Mary Ellen Weeks

TEACHING METHODS & MATERIALS

All 4s and 5s by Andrew Sharos

Boredom Busters by Katie Powell

The Classroom Chef by John Stevens and Matt Vaudrey

The Collaborative Classroom by Trevor Muir

Copyrighteous by Diana Gill

Ditch That Homework by Matt Miller and Alice Keeler

Ditch That Textbook by Matt Miller

Don't Ditch That Tech by Matt Miller, Nate Ridgway, and
    Angelia Ridgway

EDrenaline Rush by John Meehan

Educated by Design by Michael Cohen, The Tech Rabbi

The EduProtocol Field Guide by Marlena Hebern and Jon Corippo

The EduProtocol Field Guide: Book 2 by Marlena Hebern and
    Jon Corippo

Instant Relevance by Denis Sheeran

LAUNCH by John Spencer and A. J. Juliani

Make Learning MAGICAL by Tisha Richmond

Pure Genius by Don Wettrick

The Revolution by Darren Ellwein and Derek McCoy

Shift This! by Joy Kirr

Skyrocket Your Teacher Coaching by Michael Cary Sonbert

Spark Learning by Ramsey Musallam

Sparks in the Dark by Travis Crowder and Todd Nesloney

Table Talk Math by John Stevens

The Wild Card by Hope and Wade King

The Writing on the Classroom Wall by Steve Wyborney

CHILDREN'S BOOKS

Beyond Us by Aaron Polansky

Cannonball In by Tara Martin

Dolphins in Trees by Aaron Polansky

I Want to Be a Lot by Ashley Savage

The Princes of Serendip by Allyson Apsey

The Wild Card Kids by Hope and Wade King

Zom-Be a Design Thinker by Amanda Fox